Weapons of
the Waffen SS

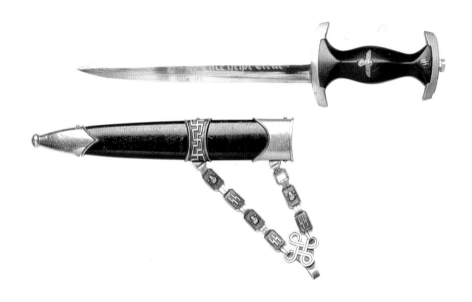

WAFFEN-SS

EINTRITT NACH VOLLENDETEM 17. LEBENSJAHR

Weapons of
the Waffen SS

David Fleming

MBI

This edition first published in 2003 by MBI Publishing Company, Galtier Plaza, Suite 200, 380 Jackson Street, St. Paul, MN 55101-3885 USA

The information in this book is true and complete to the best of our knowledge. All recommendations are made without any guarantee on the part of the author or publisher, who also disclaim any liability incurred in connection with the use of this data or specific details.

We recognize that some words, model names, and designations, for example, mentioned herein are the property of the trademark holder. We use them for identification purposes only.

This is not an official publication.

MBI Publishing Company books are also available at discounts in bulk quantity for industrial or sales-promotional use. For details write to Special Sales Manager at Motorbooks International Wholesalers & Distributors, Galtier Plaza, Suite 200, 380 Jackson Street, St. Paul, MN 55101-3885, USA.

Library of Congress Cataloging-in-Publication Data Available

ISBN: 0 7603 1594 9

Credits:
Project Manager: Antony Shaw
Art Director: John Heritage
Designers: Q2A Solutions
Indexer: John Rutter
Reproduction: Anorax Imaging Ltd

On the front cover: A Waffen SS soldier, with a fighting knife wedged between his bandoliers of ammunition.

On the half-title page: A 1936-pattern SS chained dagger.

On the title page: A Waffen SS recruiting poster from 1941, and a SS general officer's field cap with aluminium piping and insignia of zinc alloy.

On the back cover: Men of the 'Hitlerjugend' Division beside a 7.5cm Pak 40 anti-tank gun in Normandy, 1944; 9mm Pistole P 08 (Luger).

Printed in Taiwan

Contents

1 History

The origins of the SS dated back to the early 1920s when Adolf Hitler decided to raise a force to act as a counter to his brown-shirted Sturmabteilungen or storm groups.

Above: Heinrich Himmler (left) and Ernst Röhm, leader of the Sturmabteilung (SA), at a ceremony in August 1933. Within a year Röhm would be dead, killed by Himmler's SS executioners, and the SA relegated to a secondary role in the Nazi Party regime.

In contrast to the Sturmabteilungen (SA), with its drunken and brawling thugs, the SS (Schutzstaffeln, or protection squads) was to be a tightly knit, highly motivated organization that would provide Hitler with a bodyguard and act as a spearhead in the Nazi rise to power.

Under the leadership of Heinrich Himmler (appointed Reichsführer SS on January 16, 1929) the SS expanded steadily from an original nucleus of just 200 men in 1923. With the Nazi accession to power in 1933 the requirement for a bodyguard to perform ceremonial functions was considered necessary. Accordingly, on March 17, 1933, the Führer ordered the formation of a headquarters guard under the command of his former personal bodyguard and chauffeur, Josef 'Sepp' Dietrich. In this Stabswache (staff guard) of just 120 carefully selected personnel lay the genesis of the infamous Waffen (armed) SS.

In September 1933 these guardsmen received the official title of Leibstandarte SS 'Adolf Hitler', and on November 9 they swore a solemn oath that bound them unconditionally to the Führer—and to him alone. At a stroke Hitler had created a new praetorian guard that stood outside the German state, its only law to slavishly obey the commands of its 'emperor'. Kitted-out in dramatic black full-dress uniform, the men of the Leibstandarte escorted Hitler during his official functions and acted as his guard at the Chancellery.

The Leibstandarte was not the only armed SS unit, however. During 1933–34 SS 'political action squads' were formed in a number of major cities throughout Germany. Organized along similar lines to that of the Leibstandarte, they were given the title of SS Verfügungstruppen (SS-VT) and swiftly grew to a size of two standarten (regiments). The third element of the armed SS was supplied by the guards who ran the rapidly expanding system of political prisons and concentration camps; they were known by their appropriately sinister title of SS Totenkopfverbände (death's-head detachments).

The first test for the SS came with the elimination of the SA leadership. Once in power, Hitler had dropped the revolutionary rhetoric of the Nazi Party's street-fighting days, whereas the SA radicals wanted to push things further in a program that would have included the replacement of the German Army by an SA militia. Horrified at the prospect, the Army promised its full support for Hitler in exchange for a monopoly of the 'right to bear arms' and for the crushing of the SA as a political force. Keen to prove themselves and to gain the ascendancy over the SA, Himmler's armed SS made ideal executioners.

Below: The 1st Company of the Leibstandarte 'Adolf Hitler' is prepared for inspection, November 1935. The soldier on the far left, Theodor Wisch, commanded the Leibstandarte Panzer Division during the Normandy battles of 1944.

Above: A trumpeter of the Leibstandarte blows a fanfare during celebrations in 1933, the year of Hitler's rise to power.

⚡ Night of the Long Knives

In the weeks following June 30, 1934, while the secret police rounded up unsuspecting SA leaders (including its chief Ernst Röhm), the execution squads of the SS killed their former political comrades in arms. The 'blood purge' of 1934 was a turning point for the SS; they were now the undisputed 'political soldiers' of the Reich, elevated to the status of an independent organization within the Nazi Party by Adolf Hitler's decree of July 26, 1934. Ironically, the Army's price for the ending of the SA threat included the acceptance of the SS as a separate armed force. Although the SS appeared to pose no threat to the Army's pre-eminent position in 1934, the Führer's decree was to sow the seeds of a bitter rivalry.

⚡ Recruiting an Elite

The recruitment policies of the SS during the 1930s placed great importance on maintaining racial purity: extensive documentation of a sound Aryan pedigree was essential for the successful recruit. Standards of physical excellence were equally important and evidence of any minor medical complaint could be enough to bar the applicant. In an attempt to break down the traditional class barriers that were such a feature of the German Army, the SS encouraged recruits from all social backgrounds and formal educational qualifications were largely dispensed with.

Himmler saw the SS as a modern reincarnation of the chivalric orders of the Middle Ages and even went so far as instituting an Arthurian Round Table, complete with spurious coats of arms for favored officers who met regularly at the Reichsführer's castle at Wewelsburg in eastern Westphalia. Daggers and signet rings were also provided as coveted symbols of SS exclusiveness. The process was completed with a mass initiation ceremony, involving torch-lit parades and a binding oath to Hitler.

When Hitler formally reintroduced conscription and decreed the expansion of the Army on March 16, 1935, he also issued an order to increase the size of the armed SS, which then comprised the Leibstandarte, the two standarten ('Deutschland' and 'Germania') of the SS-VT, and the Totenkopfverbände. Himmler would have liked to dramatically expand the armed SS as a whole but Hitler moderated his demands in the face of determined Army opposition, although following the annexation of Austria in March 1938, a new SS-VT standarte, 'Der Führer', was raised (largely from Austrian recruits).

By 1939 the SS-VT consisted of three standarten (plus the Leibstandarte) with full supporting arms, including two motorcycle battalions along with communications and pioneer battalions. As the threat of war became ever more certain during the summer of 1939, the nucleus of an elite SS fighting force was beginning to emerge.

Left: Himmler, Hitler and senior SS officers take up a vantage point to look at the elite 'Deutschland' Standarte on exercises at Münsterlager, May 1939. Both Himmler and Hitler took a close interest in the activities of the armed SS.

⚡ *Waffen SS at War*

The invasion of Poland on September 1, 1939, provided the armed SS with their first opportunity to show their military skill, but the results were inconclusive. The SS were spread out among regular Army formations, which often showed little interest in exploiting their abilities to the full. Although the SS fought with vigor, the Army criticized their tactical skills. The real test for the SS would lay in the forthcoming campaign in the West.

The expansion of the Waffen SS (the title 'Waffen SS' became official in February 1940) during the pause before the invasion of France and the Low Countries in May brought the Leibstandarte up to the strength of a reinforced regiment, and subsequently that of a brigade. The SS-VT was formed into a full division (SS Verfügungsdivision or SS-V), under the command of its inspirational training officer Paul Hausser. At the same time a number of Totenkopf standarten were grouped together to form a division. A third division, formed mainly from Ordungspolizei personnel (Germany's paramilitary police) and strengthened by cadres of SS-V and Totenkopf troops, also came into being. The Polizei Division was very much a second-line formation, and was armed and equipped accordingly.

As the Waffen SS underwent this rapid expansion of manpower it faced a growing problem of securing arms and equipment. The Army controlled the whole German weapons program, and had little interest in providing arms to a rival organization such as the SS. Following the success in Poland the Army had undertaken its own rapid expansion of mechanized

Left: Obergruppenführer Wilhelm Koppe salutes SS and police troops; he played an important role in the destruction of the Polish nation state following the German victory in 1939. The SS version of the national eagle badge is clearly visible on his left arm.

forces, and simply did not have the spare vehicles and artillery for the SS program.

In the 1930s, the SS had looked to foreign and other German commercial sources for weapons, but these had encompassed relatively simple infantry weapons. Now that the decision had been made to convert the Waffen SS into a mechanized force, the SS staff were forced to fight with the Army for heavier German armaments. The only other alternative lay in the newly acquired high-quality armory of Czechoslovakia, but the Army had priority there too and there was little forthcoming for the SS.

One special area of contention lay in the refusal of the German Army to accept the men of the Totenkopfstandarten as soldiers at all; requests for artillery made in May 1939 had simply been ignored by Army commanders. Another bone of contention lay in the Army's reluctance to provide all Waffen SS formations with heavy artillery. The German Army rightly mistrusted Heinrich Himmler's motives and the sole possession of such powerful weapons was jealously guarded, especially if there was to be a showdown between Army and SS in the future.

Adolf Hitler normally refused to be drawn in such interdepartmental wrangling but in March 1940 he finally accepted Himmler's entreaties for help and directly ordered the Army to supply the Waffen SS with the necessary heavy armaments. But, as ever, the Army dragged its heals, leaving the Waffen SS deeply frustrated and short of munitions as the invasion of France and the Low Countries got underway on May 10, 1940.

The Leibstandarte and the bulk of the SS-V Division were deployed in the north against Holland; they had little difficulty in overrunning the flimsy Dutch defenses so that within four days advance SS units were at the outskirts of Rotterdam. Further south, the Totenkopf Division was stationed in support of the Rommel's 7th Panzer Division. When the British counterattacked

at Arras on May 21 they cut through the inexperienced Totenkopf troops, some of whom panicked and fled the field of battle. But the tide of war lay with Germany, and as the British retreated towards Dunkirk the Waffen SS was in hot pursuit. On two separate occasions Waffen SS units massacred surrendered British troops, a revealing insight into the ruthless manner in which the SS conducted war. By the time of the French surrender on June 22, the men of the Waffen SS had been fully blooded, and with the aberration of the Totenkopf Division had proved themselves battle-ready troops.

Below:

Obergruppenführer Theodore Eicke, leader of the SS concentration camp guards and commander of the Totenkopf Division in France 1940. He was killed in action in March 1943.

⚡ The Struggle for Manpower

The armistice of June 1940 brought the fighting in France to a conclusion, but the conflict between the German Army and the SS over recruitment continued unabated. At the outset of World War II, SS recruitment was centralized under the control of SS Brigadeführer Gottlob Berger. He was an organizational genius obsessively devoted to the expansion of the SS. From the beginning, Gottlob Berger saw the Army as his main enemy and he employed any and every device to get past OKW's recruitment restrictions. In addition to the authorized yearly quota, Gottlob Berger had two other sources of manpower: firstly, young German volunteers who could be inducted into the SS before reaching military service age and, secondly, racially suitable volunteers from beyond the confines of the Reich and consequently outside the OKW recruitment system.

Despite the appeal of serving in a dashing and successful organization such as the Waffen SS, there were simply not enough German youths to fulfill SS requirements. Fortunately for Gottlob Berger, Nazi Germany's conquests across Europe had opened up a new reservoir of Volksdeutsche (people of German descent) and other 'acceptable' Aryan nationalities such as the 'Germanic' Dutch, Danes and other Scandinavians.

Gottlob Berger wasted no time in sending his recruiting officers in search of the right material. The SS Standarte 'Germania' was removed from the Verfügungsdivision (subsequently renamed 'Reich') to form the nucleus of the new and very successful 'Wiking' Division, the remainder of this formation's recruits coming from Germanic volunteers.

⚡ The Fight Against Bolshevism

The Leibstandarte and 'Reich' Division were used to great effect in the invasion of Greece and Yugoslavia, but this campaign was only a precursor to the great turning point of the war, the invasion of the Soviet Union on June 22, 1941. Exploiting their initial advantage of surprise the German armored columns advanced deep into Soviet territory with the Leibstandarte and 'Wiking' divisions impressing their Army counterparts with their aggression and skill in attack. SS Division 'Reich' distinguished itself on numerous occasions and, renamed 'Das

Above: Exhausted SS troops grab some rest during an advance. Blitzkrieg warfare imposed massive strains on men and machines alike, and in the vast expanse of Russia both reached breaking point.

Hitler who ordered his armies to stand fast, which in retrospect probably proved a sound military decision. In this phase, the Waffen SS divisions added to their reputation as dashing troops in attack with a new steadfastness in defense.

The only real SS failure occurred in the far north on the Finnish Front when SS Kampfgruppe 'Nord' was ignominiously routed in an engagement on July 2, 1941. Although it was temporarily divided up among the other units by an exasperated Army commander, Himmler persevered with 'Nord' so that a few

Below: Sturmbannführer Kurt Meyer directs operations during the invasion of the Soviet Union. Meyer was a ruthless officer who transferred from the Leibstandarte to the 'Hitlerjugend' Division, achieving notoriety for responsibility in the murder of Canadian prisoners.

Reich', it came within a few kilometers of Moscow during the final, faltering stages of the operation to secure the Soviet capital, which marked the end of the German offensive of 1941.

Completely exhausted, the Germans found that their Blitzkrieg techniques—breathtakingly successful elsewhere—had met their match in the vast expanse of the Soviet Union and the stamina of the Red Army. The vigor of the Soviet counteroffensive during the winter of 1941–42 shocked the German Army High Command, which argued for full-scale withdrawals. They were, however, overruled by

Above: Kitted out in camouflage smocks, Waffen SS troops disarm and search a captured Red Army soldier. The man on the left is armed with an MP-40 sub-machine gun.

months later it was overhauled and, following reinforcement, was upgraded to a division—ultimately as the 6th SS Gebirgs (Mountain) Division 'Nord'.

Adolf Hitler was increasingly impressed with the combat record of his 'political soldiers' and ordered the formation of the 8th SS Kavallerie Division 'Florian Geyer' in September 1942 and two new German-recruited panzer grenadier divisions (9th

SS Panzergrenadier Division 'Hohenstaufen' and 10th Panzergrenadier Division 'Frundsberg') in December. This expansion, combined with the massive replacement for the losses in the other divisions, went far beyond the OKW quotas but the Führer's direct intervention forced the Army to make concessions. Gottlob Berger, the desk-bound warrior of the SS Hauptamt (main office), had once again triumphed over the German Army.

The great German summer offensive of 1942 had begun well, but the failure to capture Stalingrad and the Soviet Union's own offensive (launched on November 19, 1942) were to prove disastrous for the Germans. By early 1943 General Paulus's Sixth Army was totally isolated in Stalingrad and was forced to surrender on February 2. Other substantial German forces in the Caucasus region also faced the grim possibility of being cut off by the speed and depth of the Soviet penetration. Although Field Marshal von Manstein, commander of Army Group South, managed to extricate his forces from the Soviet trap, the momentum of the Soviet advance prevented him from stabilizing the line. By mid-February 1943, however, Manstein sensed that the Soviet thrust had become dangerously over-extended and he launched a timely counter-attack in the Kharkov region. This threw his opponents into complete disarray and allowed the Germans time to restore order

Below: A Waffen SS cavalry patrol on a reconnaissance mission on the Eastern Front. The Waffen SS deployed a number of cavalry units; this led to the formation of the 8th SS Cavalry Division 'Florian Geyer' in 1942.

Above: *Dead Waffen SS troops lie in the snow, overrun by a Soviet attack. According to the best estimates some 180,000 Waffen SS troops were killed in World War II, with a further 400,000 wounded and 70,000 noted as 'missing'.*

to their positions in the south.

The formations spearheading the assault on Kharkov (captured on March 15) were the three divisions of the newly formed SS Panzer Corps (Leibstandarte, 'Das Reich', and 'Totenkopf') under the command of Paul Hausser. For the first time a substantial body of Waffen SS troops had fought together and the result had been a resounding victory. To Hitler, who was increasingly disillusioned by repeated Army failures and what he saw as a defeatist attitude among his generals, it was a stroke of fate. From then on the Waffen SS became one of Hitler's special concerns, and the SS soldiers in the field now received the pick of the latest weapons and equipment.

The elite SS divisions, now redesignated as full panzer divisions, acquired a new role as Hitler's 'fire fighters', sent from one danger area to another as the situation demanded. The decisiveness with which both 'Das Reich' and 'Totenkopf' were employed in throwing back Soviet assaults earned them repeated praise from the Army generals who had them under their command.

In November 1943 the Leibstandarte returned to the Eastern Front. Re-equipped with large numbers of the latest Panther tanks, it fought with Army panzer divisions to crush a Soviet armored corps and retake Zhitomir.

While the Waffen SS was locked in battle on the Eastern Front, Hitler continued to authorize the formation of new SS divisions. Short of volunteers, the SS recruiters began to enforce various forms of conscription and a substantial part of both the 'Frundsberg' and 'Hohenstauffen' divisions were drafted from the older members of the Hitler Youth, although the majority of these boys would later form a separate 'Hitlerjugend' division. In March 1943 the 11th SS Freiwilligen-Panzergrenadier Division 'Nordland' was created from Norwegian and Danish volunteers.

SS *War in the West*

By 1944 increasing numbers of German troops were being stationed in the West in preparation for the forthcoming Allied invasion. Among these troops were four high-grade Waffen SS divisions: 1st SS Panzer Division Leibstandarte 'Adolf Hitler,' 2nd SS Panzer Division 'Das Reich,' 12th SS Panzer Division 'Hitlerjugend', and the 17th SS Panzergrenadier Division 'Götz von Berlichingen'. This latter division had been formed in France toward the end of 1943 from a mixture of reserve and training units with an injection of Balkan Volksdeutsche to make up the numbers.

The 12th SS Panzer Division 'Hitlerjugend' was one of the most successful examples of Nazi utilization of the nation's human assets. In January 1943 the leadership of the Hitlerjugend (Hitler Youth)—the politicized equivalent to the Boy Scout movement—suggested to the SS that a new division could draw its manpower from the older boys of the organization. There was no shortage of Hitlerjugend volunteers imbued from early childhood with Nazi ideals, and of all the SS divisions this was by far the most fanatical: any lack of experience was compensated for by an extraordinary eagerness for combat. The leadership of the division was provided by officers and the NCOs transferred from the Leibstandarte, thereby grafting experience onto the teenage rankers' enthusiasm.

The two divisions remained in close association throughout the war. They were combined into the I SS Panzer Corps for the Normandy campaign, led by the Leibstandarte's old commander, now Oberstgruppenführer Sepp Dietrich.

When the Allies came ashore on the morning of June 6, 1944, the SS divisions were scattered across France. 'Hitlerjugend' was stationed nearest the landing site, between the Orne and the Seine, with the Leibstandarte deployed farther to the east.

Below: Field Marshal Gerd von Rundstedt inspects troops from the newly formed 'Hitlerjugend' Panzer Division, prior to the Allied invasion of 1944. Rundstedt, like most other Army generals, was impressed by the professionalism and zeal of the SS troops under his command.

'Götz von Berlichingen' was held in the Loire Valley and further south still was 'Das Reich', its units deployed in and around the small Gascon town of Montauban in southwestern France. On June 20 the SS formations in France were reinforced by the arrival of the 'Hohenstaufen' and 'Frundsberg' divisions (uprated to full panzer status) from the Eastern Front.

Throughout June and July 1944 the six Waffen SS divisions (alongside their Army comrades) struggled ceaselessly to contain the Allies in the Normandy beachhead. The Allied advantage of numbers and material strength was pitted against the Germans' superior armored vehicles and tactical skill. If the Allies controlled the sky, so the high hedgerows and confined spaces of the Normandy bocage country greatly favored the defenders. Masters in the craft of flexible defensive fighting, Waffen SS troops took a heavy toll of Allied armor. Cromwell and Sherman tanks—inadequately armored and woefully undergunned—stood little

Above: Senior officers of the 'Hitlerjugend' Division discuss the tactical situation, June 1944— from the left, Max Wunsch (commander of the panzer regiment); Fritz Witt (divisional CO) and Kurt Meyer (commander of the panzergrenadier regiment).

Right: A camouflaged PzKpfw IV moves up the battlefront in Normandy, June 1944.

chance against the high-velocity guns of the German panzers and anti-tank detachments.

Inevitably, however, the sheer material weight of the Allied war machine began to grind the Germans down. On July 31 the Americans broke out of the beachhead and, sweeping south and then eastward, threatened to encircle the Waffen SS divisions around Caen. By the middle of August a total of 19 German divisions were virtually caught in a pocket with only a small gap between Falaise and Argentan open to safety in the east.

As the Allies closed in, the remnants of the 'Hitlerjugend' held the gap open around Falaise and 'Das Reich' and 'Hohenstaufen' did the same on the southern lip of the pocket's exit. A complete disaster was averted, largely due to the efforts of the Waffen SS and although 50,000 prisoners were taken many more escaped the Allied pincers. Increasingly, while ordinary German soldiers were prepared to surrender to the Allies, it was left to the

Above: Wounded Waffen SS troops are led away into captivity in Normandy. In spite of the Germans' superior tactical skills, they were overwhelmed by the sheer weight of Allied firepower during the invasion of France.

SS to fight on. Casualties were correspondingly heavy. 'Hitlerjugend', for example, was all but destroyed as a fighting force, and by September a division that had begun the battle with over 20,000 troops had been reduced to just 600.

During the autumn of 1944, as the Allied advance began to run short of supplies, the Germans managed to stabilize the front line. This encouraged Hitler to gamble on one last offensive in the West. The Waffen SS—reorganized and reinforced as best as circumstances would allow—was ordered to spearhead this offensive in the Ardennes region, an attack that would be better known as the 'Battle of the Bulge'. Launched in December the Nazis had some initial success, due largely to bad weather preventing the Allies from using their air superiority, but growing resistance from American front-line units held up the panzers, which became involved in enormous traffic jams in the Ardennes woods. Allied reinforcements on land and in the air brought the offensive to a halt by the end of December. The battered Nazi divisions were forced to retreat to their start lines; Hitler's gamble had failed miserably.

Early in 1945 the remnants of the Waffen SS in the West were withdrawn to refit and prepare to hold back the Soviet advance in the east. While some SS

Left: *SS troops lay down their weapons in northern Italy as part of the German surrender to the Allies on 30 April 1945.*

Below: *Soldiers of the Totenkopfverbände are made to dispose of the bodies of their victims, following the Allied liberation of Belsen concentration camp in April 1945. Despite avowals to the contrary the Waffen SS was implicated in the regime of the death camps.*

units were engaged in the defense of East Prussia, the remaining Waffen SS panzer formations were deployed in Hungary in a hopeless attempt to prevent its vital oil wells from falling into Soviet hands. The main offensive began on March 6 and after some early gains it foundered against the mass of the Soviet armies, the Waffen SS units lacking sufficient reserves to maintain such an attack.

This was the beginning of the end for the Waffen SS. Disillusioned by Hitler's repeated demands for the Waffen SS to sacrifice itself in hopeless military actions, the senior commanders, led by Hitler's old comrade Sepp Dietrich, quietly ordered their troops to retreat out of Hungary. An enraged Hitler disowned Dietrich and his men, but the war was lost and apart from some last ditch fighting by (mainly) foreign SS units around Berlin the short and bloody career of the Waffen SS was over.

2 *Small Arms*

Small arms are carried by the soldier at all times.
They provide vital personal protection—and for the
infantryman they are his cutting edge in battle.

Above: The Grand Mufti of Jerusalem—an anti-British Arab leader courted by the Germans —looks through the sights of a 7.92mm Karibiner 98k during a propaganda visit to the Muslim 'Handschar' Division of the Waffen SS.

SS Rifles

The bolt-action rifle was the standard infantry weapon of all combatant nations at the outset of World War II, and despite the proliferation of other weapon types it was to remain so until 1945. For the infantryman, the bolt-action rifle had the great advantage of reliability, whatever the conditions, and for the quartermaster there was the simple fact that there were millions of these tried and tested

weapons in existence, so why change to something potentially unreliable and more expensive?

The Waffen SS, like the German Army, was armed with the 7.92mm Mauser Gewehr (Gev) 98 and its variants. This Gev 98 had equipped the Kaiser's armies during World War I and was to give excellent service during the next world war.

A development of the Mauser Modell 1888 (used so successfully by the Boers against the British in the Second Boer War) the Gev 98 was a first-rate service weapon, both accurate and reliable. It employed an internal five-round box magazine and utilized the Mauser bolt-locking system—with an extra forward lug—that improved accuracy over other, similar bolt-action rifles.

At the end of World War I the Gev 98 underwent a series of minor modifications, primarily improvements to the sights, sling swivels, and bolt handle (which could be fully turned down). This led to the somewhat confusing redesignation of the rifle as the Karabiner (Kar) 98b, for despite being called a carbine it was still the same length as the standard rifle.

During the 1930s, further modifications were made to the Gev 98. These changes were largely made to aid mass-production, and this led to the

Below: A rifle-armed and camouflaged Waffen SS sniper adopts a firing position within the branches of a pine tree; snipers could be highly effective in such defensive positions.

Karabiner 98k Rifle
CALIBER: 7.92mm
MAGAZINE: 5-round internal box
LENGTH: 43.6in (1.19m)
WEIGHT: 9.26lb (4.2kg)
MUZZLE VELOCITY: 2100 fps (640 m/s)

Above right: A 7.92mm Kar 98k with grenade launcher and sight. Immediately below the rifle is an anti-tank rifle grenade, useful against light armor. Although not particularly accurate or powerful, the rifle grenade gave the infantry some much-needed long-range firepower.

introduction of the Karibiner (Kar) 98k in 1935. The main difference between the Kar 98k and its predecessors was just the loss of a few inches in length (hence the 'k' for kurz or short), but, again, its des-

ignation as a carbine was still a misnomer as the rifle was the same length as many other service rifles, including the American Springfield and Garand. Manufactured by the million, the Kar 98k became increasingly common as the war progressed, although the other two variants continued to see front-line service right through to the end of the war.

⚡ Self-loading rifles

During the late 1930s, arms designers in Germany began looking at ideas to improve and possibly supersede the old bolt-action rifles. The idea of the self-loading rifle had been around since the early years of the 20th century. It was only in 1937, however, that the German Army began to look seriously at the means of replacing the old Mauser rifle, their interest possibly stimulated by the introduction of the Garand self-loading rifle into the United States' Army in 1936.

The two arms manufacturers Mauser and Walther proposed designs that were put in to development as the Gewehr 41 (M) and Gewehr 41 (W) respectively. The Mauser version was found to be insufficiently robust for field conditions and was rejected in favor of the Gewehr 41 (W). Gases from

the muzzle were used to drive back a piston to instigate the reloading cycle.

The 41 (W) self-loading rifle did not prove a great success in the field, however; several thousand were built and saw service with the Army and Waffen SS, almost exclusively on the Eastern Front. The rifle was heavy and ill-balanced, and needed effective weapon. The Germans had also planned a sniping role for the G 43, and all models were manufactured to receive a telescopic sight; substantial numbers were fitted with 4-power telescopic sights for use as sniper rifles, although most German snipers seem to have preferred accurized versions of the bolt-action Gew 98.

Gewehr 43 Self-Loading Rifle
CALIBER: 7.92mm
MAGAZINE: 10-round box
LENGTH: 44in (1.18m)
WEIGHT: 9.7lb (4.4kg)
MUZZLE VELOCITY: 2546fps (776m/s)

constant maintenance to operate effectively. A successor was obviously required.

On the Eastern Front, the German Army had encountered the Soviet Tokarev SVT-40 self-loading rifle that used a more conventional system of tapping off the gas from the barrel than the 41 (W) — approximately half way between chamber and muzzle, rather than from the muzzle itself. Based partly on the 41 (W), and employing the Tokarev gas-operating system, the new Gewehr 43 entered service on the Eastern Front in 1943. Although the Gewehr 43 never replaced the bolt-action Mauser rifles, this self-loading rifle proved a generally reliable and

Left: The 7.92mm Gewehr 43 self-loading rifle. Used extensively on the Eastern Front, the Gew 43 was a reliable and effective weapon, providing the foot soldier with a faster rate of fire than was possible with a bolt-action rifle.

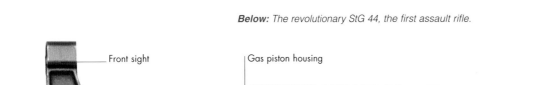

Below: The revolutionary StG 44, the first assault rifle.

Rear Sight

Front sight

Gas piston housing

Fore guard with holes to aid barrel-heat dissipation

Below: One of the more bizarre accessories for the StG 44—the Krummlauf curved barrel. This device was attached to the muzzle and was intended to direct fire around corners. Few were produced and even fewer used in action.

ᛋᛋ Assault Rifle

Following studies by the German Army of combat performance during World War I, it was found that few infantrymen used their rifles at ranges beyond 440yd (400m) but the standard rifle cartridge fired a round capable of knocking out an opponent at ranges well in excess of 1100yd (1000m). During the interwar years German small arms designers argued that a smaller, lighter cartridge, containing less propellant, would allow the infantryman to effectively engage the enemy in almost all combat situations, and yet would enable him to carry more ammunition, and, significantly, would make possible genuine automatic fire.

The standard rifle cartridge tended to be too powerful for accurate fire in automatic mode, while the pistol round fired in the sub-machine gun was only suitable for short-range combat. The solution lay in the intermediate cartridge, which was pioneered in Germany and by 1940 had led to the 7.92mm kurz (short) cartridge. This development formed the basis

Left: The Wehrmacht utilized captured stocks of the US .30 M1 carbine, giving it the designation Selbstladekarabiner (self-loading carbine) 455a. Although it only fired a light cartridge and lacked the full automatic facility of the StG 44, the light and quick-firing M1 proved popular with German troops, such as this Waffen SS soldier in the Ardennes offensive.

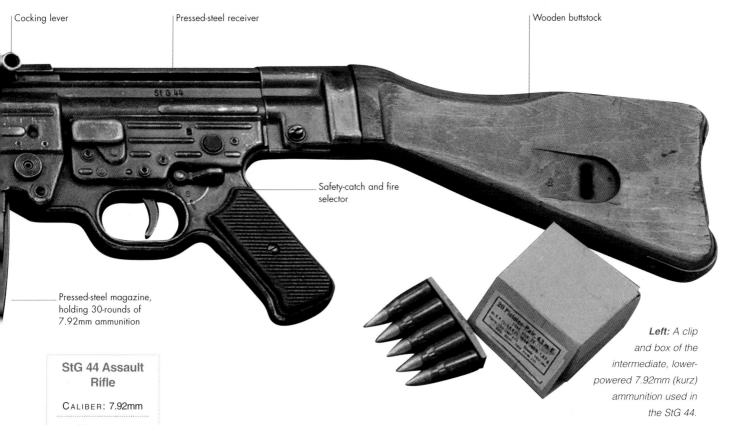

Cocking lever

Pressed-steel receiver

Wooden buttstock

Safety-catch and fire selector

Pressed-steel magazine, holding 30-rounds of 7.92mm ammunition

Left: A clip and box of the intermediate, lower-powered 7.92mm (kurz) ammunition used in the StG 44.

StG 44 Assault Rifle
CALIBER: 7.92mm
MAGAZINE: 30-round box
LENGTH: 37in (940mm)
WEIGHT: 11.27lb (5.22kg)
MUZZLE VELOCITY: 2132fps (650 m/s)
RATE OF FIRE (CYCLIC): 500rpm

for the assault rifle which dominated rifle design throughout the second half of the 20th century, and included such weapons as the Soviet AK-47 Kalashnikov series and the postwar German G3 assault rifle.

The genesis of the German Sturmgewehr (assault rifle) 44—or StG 44—was long and somewhat devious, due much to Hitler's personal refusal to allow a new rifle cartridge to be introduced into the Wehrmacht's ammunition supply system. Denied permission to develop a genuine assault rifle, Louis Schmeisser and his design team at the Haenel works quietly ignored the Führer's order and carried on with their work, concealing the weapon as a sub-machine gun with the designation of MP (Maschinenpistole) 43.

The MP 43 (subsequently redesignated StG 44 once Hitler had seen how good a weapon it was) was a revolutionary rifle. Besides providing the ordinary

infantryman with the ability to fire aimed single-shots out to 440yd (400m) it also allowed him full automatic fire at short range, thereby providing him with the advantages of rifle, sub-machine gun and, to some degree, a light machine gun. And whereas the conventional infantry rifle was an expensive, slow-to-manufacture, hand-tooled weapon, the StG 44 was a mass-produced rifle making good use of simple metal stampings and assembly line production.

German forces bitterly fighting against the mass infantry attacks of the Red Army on the Eastern Front clamored for such a weapon, and the Waffen SS units were among the first to receive the StG 44. Although possibly apocryphal, the incident which convinced the German forces on the Eastern Front of the efficacy of the new assault rifle occurred when troops cut-off by Soviet forces were parachuted a supply of the experimental StG 44s. After a swift

MP 28 Sub-Machine Gun
CALIBER: 9mm
MAGAZINE: 32-round box
LENGTH (STOCK EXTENDED): 32in (813mm)
WEIGHT (LOADED): 11.56lb (5.245kg)
MUZZLE VELOCITY: 1200fps (365 m/s)
RATE OF FIRE (CYCLIC): 500rpm

induction course the beleaguered German infantry-men shot their way out of what was a seemingly impossible position; from then on the assault rifle was the infantryman's weapon of choice on the Eastern Front. Indeed, one German report cited the weapon for its excellent reliability: 'Of all infantry weapons, the Sturmgewehr was the only one which always worked unobjectionably in Russia's dirt, cold and snow-dust, had no misfires and was resist-ant to stoppages'.

The other assault rifle in the German arms inven-tory was the Fallschirmjägergewehr (FG) 42, devel-oped on Luftwaffe direction for paratroopers, and used by the 500th and 600th Waffen SS Paratroop Battalions. The FG 42 featured a side-mounted 20-round magazine, and like the StG 44 made use of pressed-steel construction methods. But unlike the StG 44, this weapon fired the full-power cartridge which made it very difficult to fire accurately on full automatic. It was also a complex and expensive rifle to manufacture and with growing opposition from the Army to this competition for precious resources only 7000 were produced. The FG 42 was first used operationally during the raid on the Grand Sasso, where SS commandos under the leadership of Otto Skorzeny rescued the Italian dic-tator Mussolini from his mountain prison.

Right: Two Waffen SS cavalrymen engage in conversa-tion on the Eastern Front. The soldier on the right is armed with a StG 44 assault rifle, reflecting the SS's pri-ority in the allocation of this fine weapon.

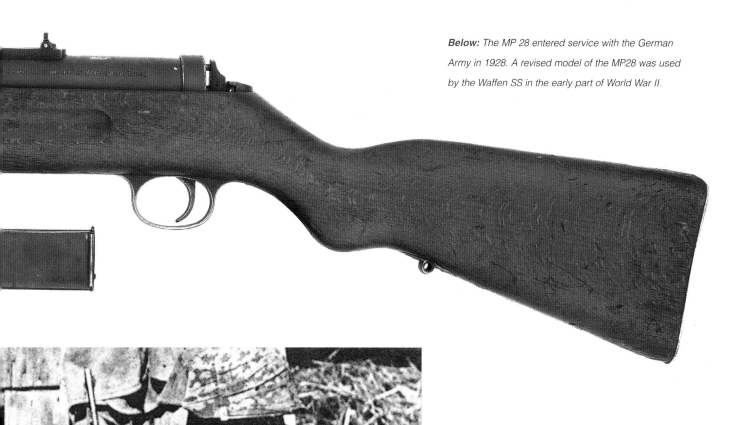

Sub-machine guns

The close-range trench fighting that typified much of the war on the Western Front during World War I led to the development of the sub-machine gun. Instead of the relatively slow-firing rifle, accurate at long-ranges, the requirement was for a short-range weapon with high firepower.

The first true sub-machine gun, the MP 18, was introduced by the Germans in 1918, and it became the model that other manufacturers were to follow. The rifle cartridge was too powerful and heavy for use in what was to be a fully automatic weapon, and so the designers turned to the only other round on offer at the time: the pistol cartridge. The MP 18 fired the standard German 9mm Parabellum pistol round, utilizing the blowback principle, where the recoil directly forced back the (unlocked) breech block to rechamber the next round.

The MP 18 was fitted with a side-mounted 32-round box magazine, and had a wooden stock and a perforated barrel sleeve to aid cooling of the barrel. Although the MP 18 was only used in limited numbers during World War I, a revised model, the MP 28, entered German Army service in 1928 and saw service with the Waffen SS in the early stages of World War II. The MP 28 featured some minor changes including new sights, the provision of a single-shot feature and a bayonet mounting.

The Waffen SS, ever on the lookout for sources of supply which would not be in direct competition with the Army, discovered a prototype sub-machine gun intended for use by the German police. This was the MP 34, which after the incorporation of a number of minor improvements became the MP 35. The weapon was similar in look to the MP 28 except that, rather unusually, the magazine feed was on the right-hand side. Reliable and accurate enough for close-combat fighting, production of the MP 35 was taken over exclusively by the Waffen SS, and considerable numbers of this weapon saw service on the Eastern Front.

While the Waffen SS was able to congratulate itself on its acquisition of the MP 35, the Army had stolen a march with the introduction of the MP 38 sub-machine gun in 1938. Although employing the basic blow-back operation of previous German sub-machine guns, the MP 38 was revolutionary in its manufacture. It marked the demise of the centuries-old gun-making traditions of labor-intensive craft manufacture using machine tooling and its replacement by basic metal stampings, die-cast parts and the use of metals or plastics instead of wood.

The MP 38 was fitted with a folding steel stock so that the sub-machine gun could be used in the confines of an armored vehicle; it was also fitted with a lip on the lower part of the barrel near the muzzle to act as a firing rest from vehicle loopholes. Unlike the

MP 28 and MP 35, the MP 38 had a magazine fitted underneath the body, capable of carrying 32 rounds. Once in service, the Army asked for a number of revisions and the possibility of even cheaper and quicker manufacturing methods. This led to the MP 40. The construction was simplified even further and a new cocking handle was introduced which locked the bolt forward and prevented any inadvertent discharge should the weapon be accidentally dropped on its butt.

The MP 38 and MP 40 became the German armed forces' standard sub-machine gun and came to personify the aggressive spirit of Blitzkrieg. Given the demand for this weapon, and the fact that German industry could never meet demand, the Waffen SS initially had difficulty guaranteeing supplies, but as the war progressed and the Waffen SS's star ascended so sources opened up to them.

But as always, the chronic German weapon shortage ensured that captured sub-machine guns were pressed into service by the Waffen SS. On the Eastern Front, the Germans first encountered the Soviet 7.62mm PPD, which owed much to the Finnish Suomi M1931 and the German's own MP 28. Featuring a wooden stock and a 71-round drum magazine, Waffen SS troops came across many captured examples as they pressed eastwards in the opening stages of Operation Barbarossa.

More prized still was a development of the PPD, the 7.62mm PPSh-41. They were eagerly sought by Waffen SS troops who found they could fire their own 7.63mm Mauser pistol rounds with this gun as well as standard captured Soviet ammunition. The appeal of the PPSh-41 was its ruggedness in the unforgiving conditions encountered in Russia; where other weapons might freeze from cold or be blocked by mud, the PPSh-41 fired on. The Germans were so impressed by the Soviet weapon that they even rechambered some captured examples to take their standard 9mm sub-machine gun round.

Right: The Machine Pistol 1940 (MP40) Schmeisser, 9mm, with canvas magazine pouches.

Right: *The P.08 9mm semi-automatic pistol— with open toggle and a box of ammunition.*

⚡ Pistols

Although large numbers of pistols were issued to the German armed forces, few were used in actual combat. For the most part they were worn as badges of rank and prestige by officers and NCOs, or used as means of coercion and control by military police-men. Lacking in range and accuracy, they compared poorly with the other small arms available to the infantryman. Nonetheless, the German arms indus-

try produced a fine range of military pistols, and they were avidly taken up by the Waffen SS.

A 9mm semiautomatic pistol was developed by Walther in the 1930s and was offered to the German Army, which accepted the weapon as the Pistole '38 (P 38). Rugged and reasonably accurate it was a first-rate military weapon, and as ever with the German arms industry the problem was to meet

Left: *Waffen SS troops pose with American cigarettes in front of an abandoned US tank destroyer. The soldier on the far left is holding a captured 9mm Browning GP 35 and has a fighting knife wedged between his bandoliers of ammunition.*

Walther P 38 Pistol

CALIBER: 9mm

MAGAZINE:
8-round box

LENGTH:
8.58in (218mm)

WEIGHT:
2.12lb (960g)

MUZZLE VELOCITY:
1150 fps (350 m/s)

Above: The standard German pistol of World War II, the 9mm Walther P 38. An excellent weapon, the P 38 saw widespread service with many armed forces in the post-war period.

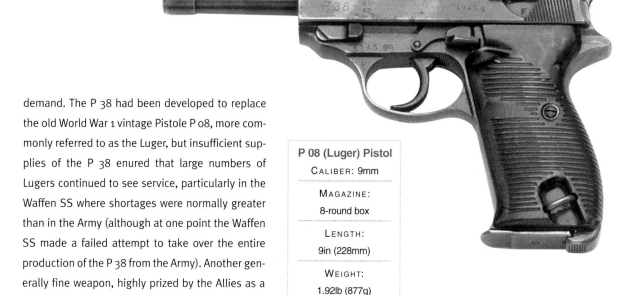

demand. The P 38 had been developed to replace the old World War 1 vintage Pistole P 08, more commonly referred to as the Luger, but insufficient supplies of the P 38 enured that large numbers of Lugers continued to see service, particularly in the Waffen SS where shortages were normally greater than in the Army (although at one point the Waffen SS made a failed attempt to take over the entire production of the P 38 from the Army). Another generally fine weapon, highly prized by the Allies as a trophy in both world wars, the P 08 was let down by a cumbersome toggle action which was expensive to produce and liable to breakdown in the field.

P 08 (Luger) Pistol

CALIBER: 9mm

MAGAZINE:
8-round box

LENGTH:
9in (228mm)

WEIGHT:
1.92lb (877g)

MUZZLE VELOCITY:
1250 fps (381 m/s)

Above: The 9mm Pistole P 08 (Luger), one the most famous hand guns of the 20th century. The was weapon produced for service during World War I.

The overall shortage of pistols forced the SS to look for other sources, both at home and abroad. In Germany they secured limited numbers of the Walther PP and PPK pistols.

The PP had been developed for general police use and considerable numbers had been allotted to the 4th SS Police Division and to other police elements within the SS. Especially popular with SS officers was the shorter-barrelled PPK, which had been designed for undercover work so that it could be carried in a pocket or under the shoulder. Both pistols were excellent designs, although intended for short-range work under 10 yards (9 meters) they had limited military use.

Another unusual weapon that found its way into SS hands was the old Mauser C 96. This was nicknamed the 'broomhandle' Mauser because of its distinctive pistol grip. Bulky and overly complex it nonetheless was a popular acquisition among Waffen SS troops, partly for reasons of prestige and simple rarity value.

Below: The 7.63mm Mauser M96 pistol, complete with its wooden holster/stock and a clip of ammunition. Despite its 19th-century origins, it was used by the Waffen SS during the early years of the war.

Foreign weapons included the 9mm Browning GP 35 manufactured by the Belgian FN company, which was overrun by the Germans in 1940. Designated the Pistole P620(b) this was one of the best military pistols of the war and stocks of this weapon were eagerly seized by the Waffen SS—although once again these were not sufficient to meet demand. Other pistols used by the Waffen SS included the 9mm Polish Radom, based on a Browning design and redesignated the Pistole 35(p) and two Czech designs which became the 7.65mm Pistole 27(t) and the 9mm Pistole 39(t).

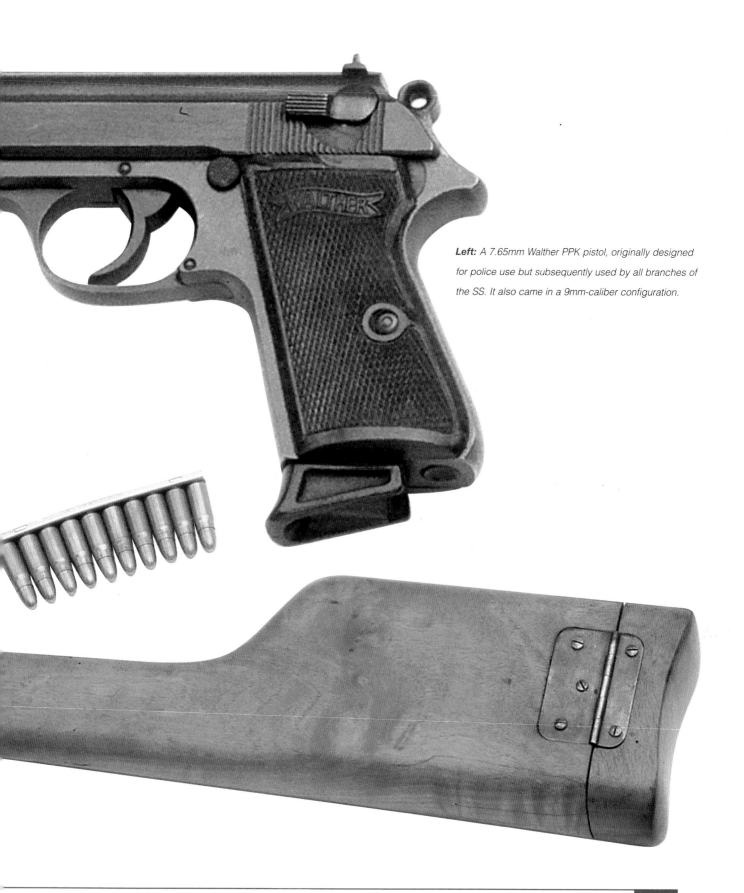

Left: *A 7.65mm Walther PPK pistol, originally designed for police use but subsequently used by all branches of the SS. It also came in a 9mm-caliber configuration.*

3 *Infantry Support Weapons*

The rifle-armed infantryman remained the mainstay of the battlefield in World War II but he increasingly relied upon an array of support weapons to provide extra firepower.

Top: Wearing old-pattern steel helmets—from World War I—a Waffen SS gun crew fires a 1908-pattern machine gun, also from World War I.

SS *Machine guns*

During World War I the machine gun—belt-fed, tripod-mounted and water-cooled—became one of the dominant weapons on the battlefield. These machine guns, however, were heavy and lacked maneuverability. While machine guns, such as the British Vickers or German Maxim, were ideal for defensive fighting from fixed positions, these were not so effective in offensive operations. During the course of the war a solution to this problem was found in the light machine gun, an air-cooled weapon mounted on a simple bipod, firing 30-or-so rounds from a box magazine. In order to prevent the barrel from overheating, it had a quick-change mechanism so that the barrel could be replaced at regular intervals, which also prevented undue wear while maintaining accuracy.

Left: A MG 34 gun crew in action. This MG 34 is mounted on a Dreifuss anti-aircraft tripod, although it is being used in a ground-fire role.

MG 34 Machine Gun

CALIBER: 7.92mm

AMMUNITION FEED:
50/250-round belt or
75-round saddle drum

LENGTH:
48in (1.22m)

WEIGHT:
25.4lb (11.5kg)

MUZZLE VELOCITY:
2500fps (762m/s)

RATE OF FIRE
(CYCLIC):
800-900rpm

Right: Troops of the SS Polizei Division await the order to fire a MG 34 machine gun during the invasion of France, 1940. While the NCO (left) uses his binoculars to search for targets the 'Number Two' ensures that the belt of 7.92mm ammunition will not jam when the gun is fired.

flash hider

front sight

barrel

perforated
barrel jacket

bipod

MG 42 Machine Gun	
CALIBER: 7.92mm	
AMMUNITION FEED: 50/250-round belt	
LENGTH: 47in (1.20m)	
WEIGHT: 25.6lb (11.6kg))	
MUZZLE VELOCITY: 2500 fps (762 m/s)	
RATE OF FIRE (CYCLIC): up to 1550 rpm	

Above: The MG 42 machine gun. The MG 42 was the best machine gun to see service during World War II. The weapon was light, accurate, reliable and reasonably easy to manufacture. It had a phenomenal rate of fire of up to 1550 rounds per minute.

During the interwar years the German Army decided against adopting the heavy machine gun/light machine gun system, and instead developed a radical new concept that subsequently became known as the general purpose machine gun (GPMG). It took the best elements from both systems: it was air-cooled (with a quick-change barrel), belt fed, and when used in a light role was mounted on its integral bipod. For sustained-fire operations it employed a tripod with optical sight.

The first of these new weapons was the MG 34, developed during the 1930s. Although predominantly a belt-fed weapon, it could also take a 75-round saddle-drum magazine for offensive opera-

tions (although it was later found that the belt system was able to withstand the rigors of the attack). The MG 34 was a superb machine gun, popular with the troops and feared by the enemy. Rugged and reliable it had a maximum range of up to 2200yd (2000m). The only criticism that could be leveled against the gun was that it was expensive and slow to manufacture. As a consequence the German arms industry could never keep up with demand.

In order to speed up production it was decided to develop an easier-to-manufacture weapon: the MG 42. This was an even better piece of equipment than the MG 34 and probably deserves the accolade of the finest machine gun ever made—today's German armed forces still use a modified version of this weapon. The MG 42 machine gun made extensive use of steel pressings although careful planning in the design stage ensured that there was no loss in overall quality.

The barrel-changing mechanism was improved, which was just as well as the MG 42 had the phenomenal rate of fire of up to 1550 rounds per minute. For the Allied infantrymen facing this

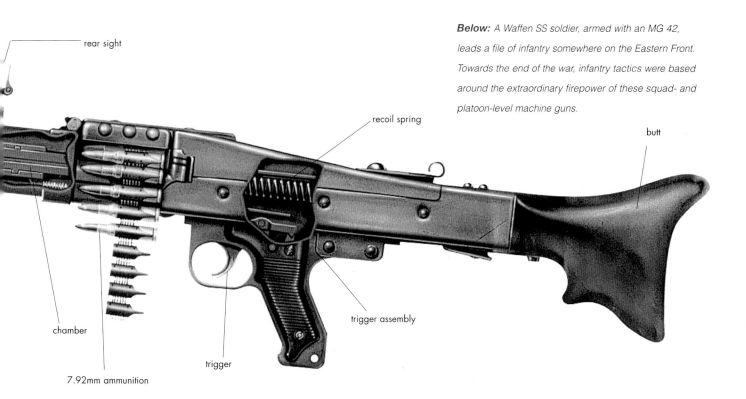

rear sight

recoil spring

Below: A Waffen SS soldier, armed with an MG 42, leads a file of infantry somewhere on the Eastern Front. Towards the end of the war, infantry tactics were based around the extraordinary firepower of these squad- and platoon-level machine guns.

butt

chamber

trigger assembly

7.92mm ammunition

trigger

Above: An exhausted-looking SS soldier carries an MG 42 machine gun during the fighting in France in 1944. The soldier's machine gun is fitted with the old saddle magazine, designed to protect the ammunition belt from dirt and snagging during operations in rough terrain.

weapon the awesome sound of an MG 42 was reminiscent of a buzz saw starting up, so fast was its rate of fire. In the hands of inexperienced troops an MG 42 could have caused a massive waste of ammunition, but under the control of the veteran Waffen SS troops manning the line in Normandy or on the Eastern Front it was a superb tool to lay down mass fire on selected spots.

Before the outbreak of war, Waffen SS units could never secure enough MG 34/42s and had to supplement their inventory with foreign models. During the 1930s the Waffen SS had been forced to rely on old water-cooled machine guns from the previous world war for training purposes. Small numbers of the Swedish 6.5mm Knorr-Bremse LH33

were bought by the SS, and rechambered to take the standard 7.92mm round it became the MG 35 — but it was never considered a weapon of choice. More successful, however, were a series of Czech light machine guns that were acquired by the Waffen SS when Germany took over Czechoslovakia in early 1939.

The ZB vz. 26 and the slightly improved ZB vz. 30 —fortunately, for the Germans, chambered in 7.92mm caliber—were used by several SS units in the early stages of the war under the designation MG 26(t) and MG 30(t). They were excellent light-machine guns (the prototype for the British Bren Gun) and their only fault was the time taken in constructing them. They remained in production under

Right: Polizei Division troops keep watch in a bunker armed with the Czech-made ZB vz. 30 light machine gun.

Below: The loader prepares to drop the shell into the barrel of a 5cm Granatwerfer 36. Although an attempt to provide the infantry platoon with its own 'artillery', the GrW 36 lacked the necessary range and weight of shell to be useful in combat conditions.

German control to meet orders from customers such as the Waffen SS, but in the end LMGs were not part of the German machine-gun philosophy. A third Czech machine gun was the 7.92mm ZB vz. 37, a tripod-mounted, air-cooled medium machine gun (the prototype of the Besa machine gun used in British tanks). Not in the same league as the MG 34, it was handed over to second-line Waffen SS formations such as the 'Prinz Eugen' Mountain Division and the 'Florian Geyer' Cavalry Division.

The final source of captured machine guns of any note came as a result of Operation Barbarossa. Vast stocks of machine guns and ammunition fell into Waffen SS hands as the Germans overran western Russia and the Ukraine during the summer and fall of 1941. They included the 7.62mm Degtyerev DP light machine gun, which utilized a 47-round, top-loaded drum magazine; the 7.62mm SG 43 medium machine gun; and the 12.7mm DShK 1938 heavy

machine gun which came complete with a wheeled carriage and small splinter shield.

SS *Mortars*

In the German armed forces the mortar was second only to the machine gun as the most important of infantry support weapons. Dubbed the foot soldier's artillery, mortars provided the infantry company (or even platoon) with an ability to lay down fire without reference to the batteries of the divisional artillery regiment, inevitably further to the rear and often with differing priorities.

The mortar was a simple, relatively light weapon and while it would never have the accuracy of an artillery piece its high rate of fire made it very effective in suppressing enemy movement. The Allied forces certainly found the German mortar arm most disconcerting; according to one report of reactions to coming under fire among British infantrymen it

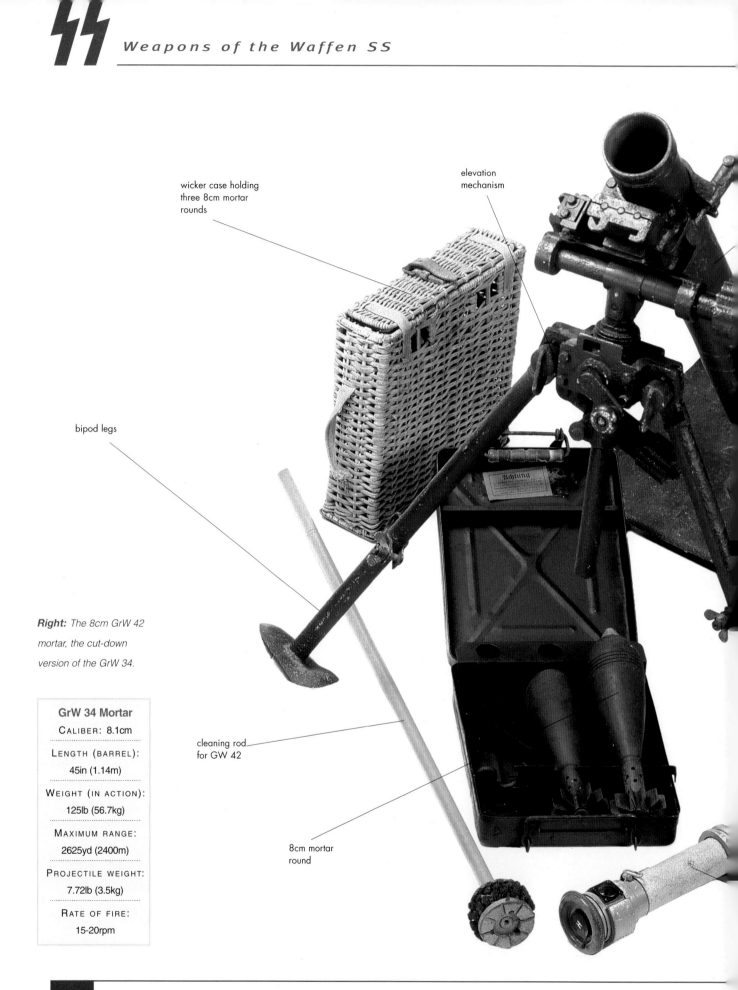

wicker case holding
three 8cm mortar
rounds

elevation
mechanism

bipod legs

Right: *The 8cm GrW 42
mortar, the cut-down
version of the GrW 34.*

cleaning rod
for GW 42

8cm mortar
round

GrW 34 Mortar
CALIBER: 8.1cm
LENGTH (BARREL): 45in (1.14m)
WEIGHT (IN ACTION): 125lb (56.7kg)
MAXIMUM RANGE: 2625yd (2400m)
PROJECTILE WEIGHT: 7.72lb (3.5kg)
RATE OF FIRE: 15-20rpm

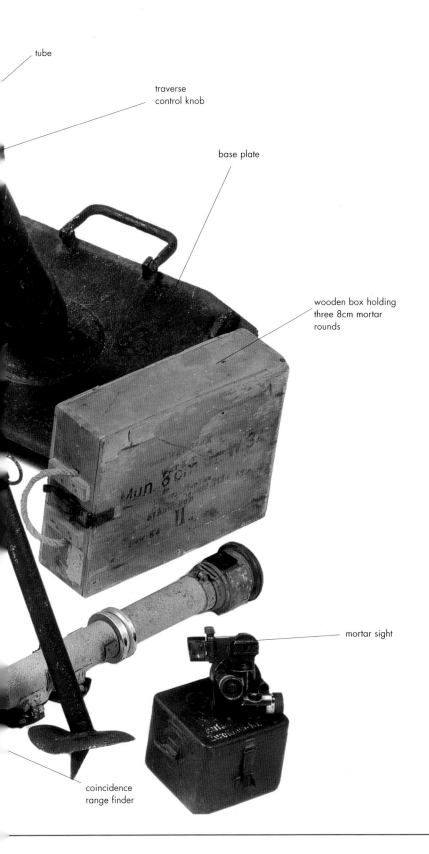

tube

traverse control knob

base plate

wooden box holding three 8cm mortar rounds

mortar sight

coincidence range finder

was only sniper fire that was more dreaded than the fall of mortar bombs.

The smallest mortar employed by the Waffen SS was the 5cm Granatwerfer (GrW) 36. This was intended as a light mortar for the rifle platoon. A well-made weapon, it was, however, considered too complex by the infantrymen using it (as well as being expensive to manufacture), and the range and payload was insufficient, being just 550yd (500m) and just under 2lbs (908g) respectively. By 1941 the Granatwerfer 36 had largely been phased out of front-line service in preference to the 8cm Granatwerfer (GrW) 34 (actual caliber 81mm), which had become the standard infantry mortar of the German armed forces.

Based on the French 81mm Brandt mortar, the GrW 34 was not a particularly advanced weapon but was rugged and reliable, and with a decent range of 2635yd (2400m) it was popular with its highly trained German crews. As well as the standard rounds of high explosive and smoke, the mortar was provided with an illuminating round to act as a marker for ground-attack aircraft. More unusual still was the Wurfgranaten 38/39, in effect a 'bouncing bomb' which contained a small charge in the head of the mortar round. This exploded on impact, sending the shell back up into the air where the main charge detonated (about 20ft up) to blast fragments all over the target area.

During the war, a new lighter version of the GrW 34 was introduced as the 8cm Kurz GrW 42 'Stummelwerfer'. The shorter barrel and lighter baseplate and bipod almost halved the mortar's weight, although the range was also halved. For the front-line soldiers this loss of range was acceptable given the 8cm GrW 42's greater maneuverability, and 'Stummelwerfer' became increasingly common on the battlefield.

During the invasion of the Soviet Union in 1941, the German forces came across the Soviet 120mm

Right: Waffen SS troops use a pontoon section on two inflatables to carry a 7.5cm IG18 light infantry gun across a river.

mortar and were immediately impressed with its ability to lay down what was in effect a miniature artillery barrage at ranges in excess of 6000yd (6600m).

Captured mortars were adopted for service by the German forces under the designation GrW 378(r), although the Nazis manufactured their own copy of the weapon as the 12cm GrW 42. Heavy by the standards of the ordinary infantry mortar, the 12cm GrW 42 utilized a simple wheeled transporter that made it relatively easy to bring in and out of action. With a rate of fire between 10 and 15 rounds-per-minute, and utilizing a good-sized 34.8lb (15.7kg) shell, a battery of four mortars could lay down a high volume of fire in a very short period.

▦ Infantry guns

Following on from their studies of the lessons to be learned from World War I, the German staff decided that the infantry should have their own lightweight artillery. This led to the introduction of the 7.5cm leichte (light) Infantry Gun (leIG) 18 and the 15cm schwere (heavy) Infantry Gun (sIG) 33.

The leIG 18 had a rather elaborate breech mechanism but otherwise was a straightforward weapon with a short barrel—capable of a maximum range of 3880yd (3550m)—and a box trail, its wheels fitted with either metal rims or rubber tires depending on whether it was horse or motor drawn (throughout the war the German armed forces relied heavily on

Right: *A selection of mines used by the Waffen SS. Left column, from top: wood box mine 42; Teller mine 42; non-magnetic Topf mine. Right column, from top: Teller anti-tank (mushroom) mine; Teller mine 35.*

horse transport). Light and relatively handy, the leIG 18 could keep up with the infantry in all but the roughest terrain. At the outbreak of war the motorized infantry regiments of the Leibstandarte, 'Deutschland', 'Germania' and 'Der Führer' were equipped with a gun company of eight leIG 18 infantry guns. One variant, issued to mountain units, was the 7.5cm Gerbig leIG 18, which dispensed with the splinter shield and could be broken down into six separate loads for mule transport or ten manpack loads.

The 15cm sIG 33 had the great advantage of being able to lob a heavy 83.8lb (38kg) high-explosive shell to a distance of 5140yd (4700m). Although this weight of shell was virtually unknown outside of artillery circles, the gun itself was too heavy and cumbersome for effective infantry use. It was only when the entire weapon was mounted on a tracked chassis that it could really advance alongside the foot soldier. Towards the end of the war, the IG 33 began to be superseded by the 12cm heavy mortar, which was far lighter and maneuverable.

⚡ Mines

As the Waffen SS was increasingly forced on the defensive from 1943 onwards so defensive weapons such as the mine were used in increasing numbers. There were two broad types of mine: anti-personnel and anti-tank. Anti-personnel mines were designed to cause maximum injury to the enemy foot soldier, and included the S-Mine—dubbed the 'shoe mine' by the Allies—which, when actuated, sprang out of the ground to waist height before detonating its shrapnel-filled canister. Another ingenious device was the Glasmine 43, in which the casing was made entirely from glass so that it could not be located by metal detectors.

The Waffen SS employed a variety of anti-tank mines. The most common mine in the early stages

of the war was the famous Teller-Mine (TMi) 35 filled with 11lb (5kg) of TNT, sufficient to disable a tank or other armored vehicle. From 1943 onward the TMi 42 series became increasingly common; this was a simpler mine to manufacture but even more effective against enemy armored vehicles.

⚡ Hand grenades

The famous stick grenade or Steilhandgranate (StG) 39 was the standard hand grenade carried by Waffen SS troops during World War II. Filled with 7oz (200g) of TNT it relied upon explosive blast rather than the effect of fragmentation, although a fragmentation sleeve could be slipped over the head of the grenade. Thrown over arm, the StG 39 had a good range of at least 30yd (28m), although one SS soldier was credited with the amazing feat of hurling a stick grenade to 77yd (70m)!

The Eihandgranate 39, or egg grenade, was considerably smaller and lighter than the stick grenade, although it contained only slightly less explosive— 6oz (170g). Like the StG 39, the EiG 39 relied on blast although again it too could take a fragmentation sleeve. As the fighting turned to the defensive

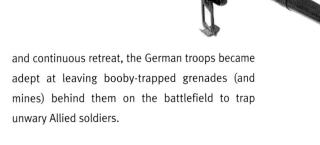

and continuous retreat, the German troops became adept at leaving booby-trapped grenades (and mines) behind them on the battlefield to trap unwary Allied soldiers.

Anti-tank weapons

From its introduction on the battlefield in 1916, the tank became a particularly fearful weapon for the infantry, and efforts were made to provide them with weapons to combat this menace. During the 1930s anti-tank rifles entered service in most European armies, the Germans adopting the 7.92mm Panzerbüsche 39. This high-velocity rifle— 4150 fps (1265 m/s)—fired a tungsten-cored bullet that could penetrate 1in (25mm) of armor plate at 330 yards (300 meters), but the increasing thickness of tank armor rendered it obsolete as early as the 1940 campaign in the West.

The solution to the infantryman's dilemma of finding a light put powerful anti-tank weapon lay in the hollow-charge principle, where the explosive is formed into an inverted cone and when detonated the blast is focused into a narrow stream of metal and gas which cuts a hole through the armor. The first such German weapon to utilize this system was the Panzerfaust 30.

This was a lightweight disposable launcher which fired a 1.5lb (680g) projectile to a range of 33yd (30m). The weapon was capable of penetrating 5.5 inches (140mm) of armor at a a 30-degree slope. The Panzerfaust 30 went into service in October 1943 and, in the hands of resolute Waffen

Above: A 7.92mm Panzerbüsche 39 anti-tank rifle, and a selection of stick grenades.

Below: This SS soldier holding a Panzerfaust 60 at a tram stop in Budapest, Hungary, November 1944.

only in limited quantities by combat engineer units. The Waffen SS had particular difficulty in obtaining flamethrowers, due mainly to Army interference, and even when supplies were secured its use was only sporadic. Although the flamethrower was the ultimate terror weapon—which could make men surrender in defended positions like no other—it was heavy and ungainly and had a very limited supply of propellant. The Flammenwerfer 35 weighed 79lb (35.8kg) and had a duration of fire of just 10 seconds (typically 10 one-second bursts) with a maximum range of 30yd (28m). The flamethrower was arguably more effective when mounted on a light vehicle, where a large tank could ensure much greater duration and more powerful application. The fuel was driven by rotary or piston pumps powered directly by the engine.

Panzerfaust 60 anti-tank weapon

LENGTH (TUBE):
31.5in (800mm)

WEIGHT (TOTAL):
15lb (6.8kg)

MUZZLE VELOCITY:
148fps (45 m/s)

MAXIMUM RANGE:
66yd (60m)

ARMOR PENETRATION:
7.87in (200mm)

Above: The 'Panzerschreck' was an effective anti-armor weapon with a longer range than the Panzerfaust. The weapon was based on the US Bazooka.

SS grenadiers, it proved an immediate success against Soviet armor. As the Panzerfaust could defeat the armor on all existing Allied tanks, efforts were made to increase its undoubtedly short range, and during the course of the war the designation (and range in meters) was increased to 60, 100 and 150.

The second hollow-charge infantry anti-tank weapon was the Raketenpanzerbüchse, (RPzB) a German copy of the American bazooka that was first encountered by the Germans in North Africa. The US caliber of 2.26in (60mm) was increased to 3.46in (8.8cm) and later designs were capable of penetrating up to 6.3in (160mm) of armor out to ranges of around 164yd (150m). Like the Bazooka it had a fearsome backblast but it was capable of knocking out any Allied tank, earning itself the nickname of Panzerschreck (tank terror).

The flamethrower had been invented by the Germans during World War I and was used by them as an infantry weapon during World War II, although

Right: Armed with a Flammenwerfer 35, a flame-thrower crew prepares for action. Flamethrowers owed much to the psychological fear that fire engenders as to their practical effectiveness.

4 Artillery

*Artillery provided much of the brute firepower for a
Waffen SS division's offensive capability.*

Above: Camouflaged by the side of a wood, SS gunners load a 10.5cm leFH 18M howitzer. The muzzle brake that distinguished this variant of the 10.5cm howitzer is visible here.

⚡ Howitzers

In the ongoing military debate whether to use guns or howitzers, the German armed forces tended to favor the howitzer. While the long-barreled gun had a higher velocity and longer range, the howitzer possessed greater operational flexibility and, for any given caliber, it fired a considerably heavier projectile. As a result of analysis of conditions encoun-

tered in World War I, the German artillery arm decided on a caliber of 10.5cm (4.13in) as the optimum size for a light field howitzer. The resulting weapon, developed by Rheinmetall, entered service in 1935 as the 10.5cm leichte FeldHaubitze (light field howitzer) 18. The leFH 18 provided the bulk of the division's artillery (three battalions, each comprising three four-gun batteries), augmented by a medium artillery battalion of 12 15cm howitzers.

The 10.5cm leFH 18 was a dependable if not particularly advanced piece of equipment, firing a 32.6lb (14.8kg) shell to a range of 11,675yd (10,675m). During the war, attempts were made to upgrade performance and to reduce weight, none of which were particularly successful.

The leFH 18M, introduced in 1940, employed a more powerful charge that required the fitting of a muzzle brake, range being extended to 13,480 yards (12,325 meters). The following year, the leFH 18/40 came into service as a weight-saving exercise, combining the FH18M gun with a 7.5cm PAK 40 carriage, but the weight saved was minimal for the effort involved.

The acquisition of sufficient artillery pieces remained a particular problem for the Waffen SS in the early stages of the war, the Army being reluctant to even let them have recently acquired Czech models. But in 1940 a number of Czech artillery pieces were allotted to the 'Totenkopf' and Polizei Divisions, and they continued to supply second-line Waffen SS formations during the war with the Soviet Union. One of the more successful of the Czech field pieces was the Skoda-manufactured 100mm vz 14/19 howitzer, designated by the Germans as the 10cm leFH 14/19. This howitzer fired a 30.87lb (14kg) shell out to a range of 10,907yd (9970m), making it a useful supplement to the standard

Below: The coffin of SS chief Reinhard Heydrich is transported on a 10.5cm leFH 18 howitzer, following his assassination by Czech resistance fighters in 1942.

sFH 18 Medium/Heavy Howitzer	
CALIBER:	15cm
LENGTH:	14ft 7in (4.44m)
WEIGHT:	12,153lb (5512kg)
MUZZLE VELOCITY:	1706fps (520m/s)
MAXIMUM RANGE:	14,500yd (13,250m)
PROJECTILE WEIGHT:	96lb (43.5kg)

German 10.5cm leFH 18.

The next step up the howitzer ladder was the 15cm schwere FeldHaubitze (heavy field howitzer) 18; a battalion of three four-gun batteries was allotted to each division. Another unremarkable but effective artillery piece, the sFH 18 fired a 96lb shell to a maximum range of 14,570yd (13,325m). Originally designed to be horse-towed, the howitzer could be broken down into two separate loads (gun and carriage), although by the outbreak of war the arrival of the SdKfz 7 half-track made possible motorized towing in a far more effective single load.

On the Eastern Front the Germans came up against the Soviet 152mm gun-howitzer, whose range of 18,880yd (17,265m) easily out-ranged that of the sFH 18. Attempts were made to increase range by adding a more powerful charge, but this only encouraged increased barrel wear and strain on the recoil system. In this area of weapons production, the Germans were at least equalled, if not surpassed, by their enemies.

⚡ Guns

Although the bulk of German artillery was provided by howitzers, guns had an important role to play. Originally, the 7.5cm field gun had been considered too small a caliber to be effective on the battlefield, although production of the 7.5cm leichte FeldKanone (light field gun) 18 continued throughout the war. Firing a 12.8lb (5.8kg) shell to a range of 10,320yd (9425m) it was used to equip the Waffen SS cavalry divisions, although as the war progressed the leFK 18 was found to be a useful dual gun/anti-tank gun. It was issued to the newly established SS panzer-grenadier divisions.

An altogether more formidable weapon was the 10cm schwere Kanone (sK) 18—although its actual caliber was 10.5cm. This long-barrelled and heavy gun was capable of firing a 33.4lb (15.1kg) to a distance of 20,860yd (19,075m) and had been designed for counter-battery work and interdiction fire behind the enemy front line. Given the Army's possessive hold on artillery, the Leibstandarte was surprisingly fortunate to receive a battalion of 12 of these guns for the 1940 campaign in the West. More sK 18s were sent to the Waffen SS as the fighting on the Eastern Front intensified during 1942-43; the panzer divisions received four-gun batteries, as did the mountain division 'Nord'.

Below: This 21cm gun is probably in action somewhere in the Soviet Union . Guns played a key role in the artillery of the Waffen SS although the bulk of their armory consisted of howitzers.

Although intended for long-range indirect fire, the sK 18 was in fact used in a direct fire role at the battle of Arnhem in 1944, where the 'Hohenstaufen' Panzer Division was attempting to destroy the British paratroop positions around the main Arnhem bridge. Firing over open sights, the flat trajectory and high velocity of the sK 18 proved invaluable in shattering the buildings the British troops were using as defenses, ultimately forcing the paratroopers to surrender.

During 1943 Himmler managed to combine his SS panzer divisions into semi-autonomous army corps (a step into making the Waffen SS an independent army). This inevitably led to the introduction of corps-level troops and weapons.

The 17cm Kanone 18 was an exceptionally powerful weapon. The gun was capable of firing a 150lb shell (68kg) shell to a range as great as 32,370yd (29,600m)—or well over 18 miles (12.8km). The 17cm Kanone 18 was joined by the 21cm Mörser 18, which lacked the other gun's range—just 18,270yd (16,700m)—but fired a considerably heavier 267lb

(121kg) shell. These heavy guns came under Himmler's direct authority, and were assigned to those fronts where the Waffen SS was fighting its hardest battles.

⛭ *Mountain guns*

The Waffen SS raised a number of mountain divisions, mainly second-line formations deployed in the Balkan region (for anti-partisan duties) or on the Finnish sector of the Eastern Front. Although they received some conventional artillery they had a special requirement for mountain guns. These guns were constructed to be as light as possible, have a high angle of elevation (to fire over steep mountain ridges) and be able to be broken down into separate loads for transportation by mules (or men) over rough country.

The 7.5cm Gebirgsgeschütz (GebG) 36 was issued to the three main SS mountain divisions— 'Nord', 'Prinz Eugen', and 'Handschar'—as their

Below: A 3.7cm artillery piece is utilized by Waffen SS mountain troops in suitably rugged terrain. Although lightweight, the 3.7cm gun lacked the punching power of dedicated mountain guns.

Above: Wearing their distinctive fezzes, troops of the 'Handschar' Division crew a GebH 40 howitzer, one of the finest mountain artillery pieces ever manufactured.

light artillery element. Developed in the 1930s the GebG 36 weighed just 1654lb (750kg) and could be broken down into eight transportation loads. It was capable of firing a 12.7lb (5.75kg) shell to a maximum range of 10,010 yds (9150m).

Designed by the Austrian firm of Böhler, the 10.5cm Gebirgshaubitz (GebH) 40 was an exceptional mountain howitzer. This howitzer had a high maximum elevation of 71 degrees and a very long

barrel that helped provide it with a range of 18,380yd (16,740m). This was a far greater range than would normally be expected from a howitzer.

The 10.5cm Gebirgshaubitz 40 weighed 3660lb (1660kg). The gun could be divided up into five separate loads. In 1942 the first GebH 40 howitzers were issued to the 'Nord' and 'Prinz Eugen' Divisions, while the 'Handschar' received them the following year.

⚡ Rocket artillery

Partly as a result of the restrictions of the Versailles Treaty on the development of heavy guns, the Germans became pioneers in the field of rocket artillery (which fell outside the terms of the Treaty). During the 1930s the Germans solved the old problem of rocket instability, which had previously rendered them unsuitable as military weapons. In the new rocket, the propellant was positioned at the front, with the explosive charge at the rear. The back-blast from the ignited propellant was voided through a series of angled venturis at the rocket's base, which imparted spin to provide the necessary stability in flight.

The first rocket to enter service (in 1941) was the 15cm Nebelwerfer (NbW) 41; it was capable of firing both high explosive and smoke projectiles ('nebelwerfer' literally means smoke discharger). The launcher consisted of a number of tubes (initially six, subsequently 10) grouped together and mounted on a Pak 35/36 anti-tank gun carriage. It could fire six 75lb (34kg) rockets out to a range of 7550yd (6900m). A full salvo could be unleashed in 10 seconds, although as the tubes had to be manually reloaded it took aproximately five minutes to fire three salvos.

Rocket launchers were not precision weapons. Rather, they were used en masse to devastate a given area. They were fatal to personnel in the open and all soft-skinned vehicles, and the concussive effect on the crews of armored vehicles would have been, at the least, highly unnerving.

Each salvo produced an enormous amount of dust and smoke, with an extensive trail of smoke that made the launcher's position highly visible and vulnerable to enemy counter-battery fire. As a consequence, Nebelwerfer batteries were highly mobile and moved to new positions after a few firings.

The whole Nazi rocket-launcher program was surrounded in secrecy by the Army and it was hardly surprising that the Waffen SS had problems obtaining stocks of the weapon. By 1943, however, Himmler had managed to secure a basic supply for his troops.

Most rocket-launcher batteries were held back as corps troops, although the Leibstandarte and 'Hitlerjugend' panzer divisions were each provided with a battery of NbW 41s.

During the course of the war new and heavier rockets were introduced. The NbW 42 fired a 21cm rocket to a distance of 8590yd (7850m), although it was less accurate than the NbW 41.

The 28cm and 32cm Wurfkörper rockets lacked the range and accuracy of the nebelwerfers but their heavy payload made them very effective in street fighting where buildings had to be quickly demolished. The Waffen SS never managed to acquire enough rocket launchers, but, at the same time, it was acknowledged that rockets were always an adjunct rather than a replacement to conventional artillery pieces.

⚡ Self-propelled artillery

Once the panzer divisions had seen combat in Poland and France, it was clear that a new type of mechanized artillery piece was required; it would need sufficient speed to keep up with the tanks (providing them with almost immediate artillery support) and it would have to provide some degree of armored protection for the gun crew. Fortunately for the German artillerymen there was a ready supply of vehicles for their use in the shape of conversions of old tank chassis. By 1940 both the PzKpfw I and II tanks had been rendered obsolete and the Czech 38(t) was also ready for conversion. And as the war went on, so more tanks became available to act as gun platforms, whether for artillery or for tank-hunting purposes.

Left: A 15cm Nebelwerfer 41, loaded and ready for firing. This example, with six tubes, is mounted on a Pak 35/36 anti-tank gun carriage, although later combinations of ten tubes were mounted on Maultier half-tracks.

NbW 41 Rocket Launcher

CALIBER: 15cm

LENGTH:
38.6in (979mm)

WEIGHT (LOADED):
1694lb (770kg)

MUZZLE VELOCITY
(INITIAL):
1220fps (342m/s)

MAXIMUM RANGE:
7553yd (6900m)

PROJECTILE WEIGHT
(ONE ROCKET):
74.8lb (34kg)

The powerful but cumbersome 15cm sIG 33 infantry gun was an early candidate for mechanization, and as early as 1940 it was mounted on a PzKpfw I chassis. This was something of a 'lash-up', the gun riding at a very high level relative to the chassis, with armor protection being a simple three-sided shield. During the course of the war the sIG 33 would be mounted on a variety of other chassis—PzKpfw II and III and the 38(t)—ensuring that production continued until 1944.

A more significant artillery conversion was the combination of the PzKpfw II with the 10.5cm le FH 18 light howitzer. This howitzer was called the

Left: Armed with a 10.5cm howitzer a Wespe self-propelled gun advances up an incline. The gun's diminutive size, when compared with the Hummel self-propelled gun (below), is clearly evident in this photograph.

Wespe Self-Propelled Gun

CREW: Five

WEIGHT:
10.83 tons (11 tonnes)

DIMENSIONS:
length 15ft 9in (4.81m);
width 7ft 6in (2.28m);
height 7ft 7in (2.3m)

ARMAMENT:
10.5cm howitzer; 1
7.92mm machine gun

POWERPLANT:
140hp Maybach 6-cylinder
petrol engine

PERFORMANCE:
max. road speed 25mph
(40kph); max cross-country speed 12mph
(20kph); road range
125 miles (200km)

Wespe (wasp). Its range was 11,675yd (10,675m) — the same as the towed piece — and the chassis provided a good road speed of 25mph (40kph). A box-like armored structure protected the crew, although its thickness of just .4in (10mm) ensured that it was only proof against small arms and shell splinters.

Ammunition stowage was limited to just 32 rounds, and in an attempt to rectify this problem a gun-less Wespe ammunition carrier (holding an additional 90 rounds) was attached to each battery. In 1942 the Leibstandarte became the first Waffen SS formation to receive the Wespe, to be followed by 'Das Reich' and 'Totenkopf'. Each division's mechanized artillery battalion would be allocated two six-gun Wespe batteries and one six-gun Hummel battery.

The Hummel (bumblebee) was a considerably more powerful piece of self-propelled artillery. The 15cm sFH 18 howitzer was mounted on a hybrid PzKpfw III/IV chassis, its five-man crew receiving only limited protection from the steel-plate box surrounding them. The 15cm howitzer could fire a high-explosive round out to 14,570yd (13,325m). The Hummel was an excellent weapon that could keep up and provide heavy fire support to the tanks and other armored vehicles; its only major weakness was that it could carry even less ammunition than the Wespe, just 18 rounds. Each battery was supported by a howitzer-less Hummel munitions carrier, but even then ammunition stocks would inevitably run low in any sustained artillery action.

Below: A battery of 15cm Hummel self-propelled guns awaits action on the steppes of the Eastern Front. A swastika flag on the vehicle (left) is an aerial recognition device to prevent the guns being shot up by any roving Luftwaffe ground-attack aircraft—a common hazard of warfare that extends to the present day.

Hummel Self-Propelled Gun
CREW: five
WEIGHT: 23.6 tons (24 tonnes)
DIMENSIONS: length 23ft 6in (7.17m); width 9ft 5in (2.87m); height 9ft 3in (2.81m)
ARMAMENT: 15cm howitzer; 7.92mm machine gun
POWERPLANT: 265hp Maybach 12-cylinder petrol engine
PERFORMANCE: max. road speed 26mph (42kph); road range 134 miles (215km)

5 *Anti-Tank Guns*

The emergence of the tank as the dominant weapon on the World War II battlefield inevitably led to the emergence of a counter weapon, namely the anti-tank gun. Some anti-tank guns were mounted on armored vehicles as tank hunters (see chapter 8) but the majority were used as specialized artillery pieces.

⚡ *Early anti-tank guns*

When Germany went to war in 1939 its armed forces were comprehensively equipped with the 3.7cm Panzerabwehrkanone (Pak) 35/36. Each Waffen SS motorized infantry regiment had its own anti-tank company equipped with 12 guns. Introduced into service in the early 1930s the Pak 35/36 was an advanced design for its day, a lightweight, high-velocity gun capable of penetrating 1.4in (36mm) of 30-degree sloped armor plate at a range of 550yd

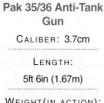

Pak 35/36 Anti-Tank Gun
CALIBER: 3.7cm
LENGTH: 5ft 6in (1.67m)
WEIGHT(IN ACTION): 723lb (328kg)
MUZZLE VELOCITY(AP): 2495 fps (760 m/s)
MAXIMUM RANGE(AP): 4400 yards (4025m)
PROJECTILE WEIGHT: 0.78lb (354g)
ARMOR PENETRATION: 1.48in (38mm) at 30 degrees at 400 yards (365m)

Below: Totenkopf troops crew a 3.7cm Pak 35/36 during a preliminary exercise for Operation Sealion—the proposed invasion of Britain in 1940.

Left: *The final attempt to upgrade the Pak 35/36 for conditions encountered in the Soviet Union - the attachment of a Stielgrenate 41 stick bomb to the muzzle of the gun.*

(500 meters)—sufficient to knock out virtually any tank in the mid 1930s.

But by 1940 the increase in armor protection of heavy tanks—notably the French Char B and the British Matilda—was beginning to expose the limitations of the Pak 35/36. During the British counterattack at Arras on May 20, 1940 their Matilda tanks sliced through the 'Totenkopf' Divison anti-tank screen, and only the timely arrival of artillery from the 7th Panzer Division—under Major General Erwin Rommel's direct command—restored order. After the battle, one broken-down Matilda was found to have taken 14 shots from Pak 35/36s without any effect.

The invasion of the Soviet Union in 1941 revealed the failings of the Pak 35/36 even further, especially after the arrival of the Red Army's T-34 tank—but by then the gun was undergoing replacement by more powerful models. While this was taking place, stopgap measures were adopted to upgrade the gun's performance.

Tungsten-carbide rounds improved penetration to a limited degree, but more effective was the employment of the 3.7cm Stielgrenate 41 stick bomb from late 1941 onward. The bomb, containing a shaped HEAT charge, was fitted over the gun's muzzle and was fired using a blank cartridge to a (very limited) distance of 330 yards (300 meters). While difficult and sometimes dangerous to use, the Stielgrenate 41 had excellent penetrative powers—up to 7.2in (180mm) of armor.

The Pak 35/36's successor was the 5cm Pak 38, which began to enter service in 1941. Like its predecessor, the gun possessed a low silhouette, but had far greater power, being able to cut through 2in (50mm) of 30-degree sloped armor at a range of 1100 yards (1000m).

Pak 38 Anti-Tank Gun

CALIBER: 5cm

LENGTH:
10ft 6in (3.18m)

WEIGHT(IN ACTION):
2205lb (1000kg)

MUZZLE VELOCITY(AP):
2903fps (835m/s)

MAXIMUM RANGE(HE):
2900yd (2650m)

PROJECTILE WEIGHT:
4.54lb (2.06kg)

ARMOR PENETRATION:
3.98in (101mm) at
820yd (740m)

⚡ *The tank killers*

Even while the Pak 38 was being distributed to the anti-tank companies of the Waffen SS formations fighting on the Eastern Front, work was in the final stages of completing the 7.5cm Pak 40 anti-tank gun. The Pak 40 (or 'Hünengrab') was an excellent compromise between power and weight, and can be viewed as one of the best anti-tank guns of the war. It could take on armored vehicles at ranges of up to 2200yd (2000m), where it could penetrate 3.86in (98mm) of armor plate. Some 23,303 Pak 40s were produced between 1942 and 1945. The Pak 38 and 40 formed the mainstay of the Waffen SS's anti-tank armory, and were generally more than a match for any Allied tanks set against them.

Some idea of the effectiveness of the Waffen-SS Pak 40s can be seen in the Operation Totalize battles of August 1944, when two Pak 40s of the 'Hitlerjugend' Division, with the divisional escort company, stopped an advance by the 1st Polish Armoured Regiment in its tracks. Despite repeated attacks by the Polish Sherman tanks, the Waffen SS gunners held their position and by the end of the engagement 22 Shermans had been knocked out.

The German arms designers were determined to produce an even more powerful anti-tank weapon, the result being the 8.8cm gun. Even before the outbreak of war, the high-velocity 8.8cm anti-aircraft gun had been found to be highly effective against enemy armor, and from 1939 onward it had been used in a dual anti-aircraft/anti-tank role. The '88' gained an awesome reputation in the Western Desert and on the Russian Steppes, but its high profile made it vulnerable to counter-battery fire.

The new Krupp-designed 8.8cm Pak 43 had superior performance and was easier to use than its Flak counterpart, and became the most powerful anti-tank gun used by the Waffen SS. It was a fatal to all enemy armor, able to take out most Allied

tanks at ranges in excess of two miles. The need for such a powerful anti-tank gun became apparent in 1944 with the arrival of the Soviet JS II heavy tank, which had a maximum armor thickness of 6.2in (160mm). The Pak 43 also fired high explosive shells, and with a range of 16,575 yards (15,150 meters) it proved a useful artillery weapon.

Expensive and complex to build and operate, the Pak 43 was not available to the Waffen SS in substantial numbers until the end of 1944 when the war was entering its final stages. A simpler and cheaper version was produced and designated the Pak 43/41. Despite its ability to carve through enemy armor like a knife through butter, the 8.8cm anti-tank gun was also heavy and difficult to maneuver — the troops called it the Scheunentor or 'barn door'. But whatever its failings in mobility, the Pak 43 and 43/41 were much feared by Allied tank crews.

Left: Men of the 'Hitlerjugend' Division wait beside a 7.5cm Pak 40 anti-tank gun during the Normandy campaign of 1944. The Pak 40 was an excellent compromise between armor penetration and maneuverability.

Pak 40 Anti-Tank Gun	Pak 43 Anti-TankGun
CALIBER: 7.5cm	CALIBER: 8.8cm
LENGTH: 12ft 2in (1.67m)	LENGTH: 21ft 8in (6.61m)
WEIGHT(IN ACTION): 3142lb (1425kg)	WEIGHT(IN ACTION): 8047lb (3650kg)
MUZZLE VELOCITY(AP): 2460fps (750 m/s)	MUZZLE VELOCITY(AP): 3707fps (1130 m/s)
MAXIMUM RANGE(HE): 8400yd (7680m)	MAXIMUM RANGE(HE): 16,570yd (15,150m)
PROJECTILE WEIGHT: 15lb (6.8kg)	PROJECTILE WEIGHT: 22.4lb (10.16g)
ARMOR PENETRATION: 3.86in (98mm) at 2200yd (2000m)	ARMOR PENETRATION: 7.24in (184mm) at 2200yd (2000m)

6 Anti-Aircraft Guns

The integration of anti-aircraft units within the ground forces of the Wehrmacht was more complete than in any other prewar army, and this attention to air defense extended to the Waffen SS.

Above: Alongside a 2cm anti-aircraft gun, a Waffen SS trooper stands guard as combat engineers reconstruct a bridge over the Veilikaya river in the Soviet Union during the summer of 1943.

From 1939–40 onward the main Waffen SS formations deployed a motorized anti-aircraft battalion, which was divided into three companies each with 12 2cm anti-aircraft guns. As the war progressed so more and heavier ordnance was distributed around the divisions, including both 3.7cm and 8.8cm guns. By 1944 a full-strength Waffen SS panzer division might expect to field anything up to 120 2cm guns (40 of them self-propelled), six quad-mounted 2cm guns, nine 3.7cm guns and 12 8.8cm guns. This formidable array of Nazi firepower was a reflection of the growing threat from Allied aircraft, especially in the West.

SS Light Flak

The 2cm Fliegerabwehrkanone (Flak) 30 had entered German service in 1935 and was used by Waffen SS units during the invasion of Poland. Manufactured by Rheinmetall-Borsig, the Flak 30 was capable of sending explosive shells to a height of 7218ft (2200m), which was a more than sufficient ceiling for its role against low-flying aircraft. Problems were, however, discovered in its magazine system, which tended to jam, and its rate of fire was subsequently considered to be too low.

An improved design was manufactured by Mauser and entered front-line service in 1940 as the Flak 38. The magazine problem was largely solved and the rate of fire increased from the 280rpm of the Flak 30 to between 420 and 480rpm. This was a substantial improvement but the German gunners were still not satisfied, especially as increases in the speed of aircraft (as well as their size and strength) required more shells in the sky at a given moment.

As a single-barrel system could not satisfactorily take any further increase in rate of fire it was decided to increase the number of barrels, so that the Flakvierling 38 comprised four barrels on a single mounting. This gave a phenomenal combined cyclic rate of fire of some 1800rpm. Of all the German AA guns, the Flakvierling 38 was the most feared by the crews of Allied low-flying aircraft. The Flakvierling was mounted on a tracked chassis—typically an SdKfz 7—which provided it with the necessary

mobility to keep up with the German panzers.

As with the famous '88', the German armed forces also used their anti-tank guns against ground targets when necessary. Although the 2cm gun was a rather small caliber, its high velocity, flat trajectory and rapid rate of fire made it a potent

Above: The four 2cm guns of the Flakvierling 38 are here mounted on a PzKpfw IV, instead of the more usual half-track chassis. When in action, the side plates would be folded down to provide a fighting platform for the gun crew.

Above: A 3.7cm anti-aircraft gun is prepared for action by Waffen SS troops on the Eastern Front.

weapon against lightly armored vehicles and minor strong points.

The requirement for a more powerful round led to the introduction of the 3.7cm Flak series. This gun not only fired a heavier projectile (five times the size of the 2cm gun) but possessed a much higher oper-ational ceiling of 15,750ft (4800m). The Flak 18 entered service in 1935 and although production stopped a year later it was used throughout the war. The Flak 18 did have a number of failings: it was slow to get in and out of action and problems with the feed mechanism led to stoppages while firing. A

The 3.7cm gun proved its worth against all but high-flying aircraft, but like so many German weapons it was a slow and expensive weapon to manufacture, and demand could not be met. As a solution, a wholly new gun was adopted by the armed forces, the 3.7cm Flak 43, which made good use of the latest production processes, including metal pressings and simpler components. As a consequence, production time was drastically cut so that four Flak 43s could be manufactured against one Flak 36/37. Rate of fire was also increased to 250rpm. A further development was the Flakzwilling 43, in which two barrels were mounted on the same platform as a means of increasing firepower (although only a small number were built before the war's end).

The heaviest anti-aircraft guns to see regular service with the Waffen SS were those of the 8.8cm Flak series. Developed with the Swedish company Bofors, the Flak 18 was first employed during the Spanish Civil War (1936–39) where its large high-velocity round was found to be particularly effective against armored vehicles as well as aircraft.

From then on the gun carried both armor-piercing and high-explosive rounds as a matter of course. An improved version–the Flak 36–featured a replaceable barrel liner and a three-part barrel assembly, while the Flak 37 had a more complete fire-control system. The 8.8cm Flak gun formed the backbone of the Waffen SS's heavy anti-aircraft complement.

As the war started, German planners were aware that the 8.8cm Flak guns would need to improve their vertical range in order to take on the latest Allied aircraft, and the result was the highly advanced 8.8cm Flak 41. The maximum effective ceiling was increased to 48,230ft (14,700m) but on the debit side this was an expensive weapon to produce and it lacked battlefield ruggedness. As a result it was only produced in limited quantities and few saw service with the Waffen SS.

replacement 3.7cm gun was developed—the Flak 36—which incorporated several modifications, making it more dependable and easier to use. The Flak 36 was joined by the Flak 37, which was essentially the same gun except with a more complex predictor sight.

Flak 38 Anti-Aircraft Gun

CALIBER: 2cm

LENGTH:
7ft 5in (2.25m)

WEIGHT(IN ACTION):
926lb (420kg)

MUZZLE VELOCITY:
2953fps (900m/s)

MAXIMUM CEILING:
7218ft (2200m)

PROJECTILE WEIGHT:
0.26lb (119g)

RATE OF FIRE
(CYCLIC):
420-480rpm

Flak 18 Anti-Aircraft Gun

CALIBER: 8.8cm

LENGTH:
25ft 0in (7.62m)

WEIGHT(IN ACTION):
11,354lb (5150kg)

MUZZLE VELOCITY:
2690 fps (820m/s)

MAXIMUM CEILING:
26,245ft (8000m)

PROJECTILE WEIGHT:
20.3lb (9.24kg)

RATE OF FIRE:
15-20rpm

7 Tanks

The tank was the dominant land weapon of World War II, and the Waffen SS would come be identified as arch exponents of armored warfare through the success of their panzer divisions.

Above: Waffen SS PzKpfw IIIs advance deep into the Soviet Union during the summer of 1942—the high-water mark of the German war in the East. Although armed with an improved 5cm gun, these Panzer IIIs were no match for the Soviet T-34.

SS First Waffen SS panzers

In 1942 the Waffen SS began to receive tanks, when they were uprated from mechanized to panzer-grenadier divisions. This change in divisional status meant that each formation was allotted its own tank battalion. During the winter of 1942–43 this transformation went a stage further.

The panzer-grenadier formations became full panzer divisions, complete with two battalions of tanks. From 1943 onward the seven elite panzer divisions of the Waffen SS would make a vital contribution to Nazi Germany's war effort, and if the final result was strategic defeat then that had to be set against a string of brilliant tactical victories by the Waffen SS—invariably against great odds.

The small and woefully undergunned tanks that Germany used to spearhead its Blitzkrieg triumphs in 1939–40 had no or little place in the story of Waffen SS armor. The Panzerkampfwagen (PzKpfw) II was the only early generation tank to see service with the Waffen SS, and that consisted of just a few reconnaissance models sent to the Leibstandarte in

1942 and withdrawn early in 1943.

The first true fighting tank to be issued to the Waffen SS was the PzKpfw III, which began to be distributed to the Leibstandarte, 'Das Reich', 'Totenkopf' and 'Wiking' in 1942. By this time the Panzer III was outclassed as a battle tank—especially when compared to the Soviet T-34—but supplies of other, more advanced designs were not then available to either the Waffen SS or the Army.

The earliest Panzer III models had been armed with a simple 3.7cm gun—the same as that of the Pak 35/36 anti-tank gun—but by 1942 it had been uprated to include a 5cm main gun. The Waffen SS received the Ausf (model) J; it was armed with a longer barreled 5cm gun (60 calibers as against the previous 42) which improved its ability to penetrate the increasingly thick armor encountered on the Eastern Front.

Equipped with a 300hp engine, the Panzer III was capable of a road speed of 25mph (40km/h) and had a generally good cross-country capability. The layout of the tank set the basic pattern for later German tanks. The driver sat in the front of the hull, on the left, with the hull machine gunner/radio operator on his right. The turret contained the remainder of the five-man crew: gunner, loader and commander, the latter having his own cupola at the top of the turret.

The Panzer III's armor protection was increased, although by early 1943 the tank had effectively reached the end of its development life. The major design block to further improvements lay primarily in its relatively small turret ring. The size of the turret ring prevented the adoption of a long-barreled

Below: A late model Panzer III with a 5cm main gun. Despite its light armor protection and the limited armor penetration of its gun, Panzer III tanks continued to see service with the Waffen SS as late as the summer of 1943.

PzKpfw III Tank Ausf L

CREW: Five

WEIGHT:
22 tons (22.3 tonnes)

DIMENSIONS:
length (inc. gun) 21ft (6.41m); width 9ft 8in (2.95m); height 8ft 3in (2.5m)

ARMAMENT:
5cm KwK 39 L/60 gun; 2 x 7.92mm machine guns (1 co-axial with main gun; 1 in hull front)

ARMOR:
hull front 2in (50mm); hull sides 1.2in (30mm); hull rear 1.2in (30mm)

POWERPLANT:
300hp Maybach 12-cylinder petrol engine

PERFORMANCE:
max. road speed 25mph (40kph); max. cross-country 15mph (24kph)

RANGE:
road 124 miles (200km); cross-country 68 miles (110km)

7.5cm gun, the minimum size needed by a battle tank from 1942 onward.

Panzer IIIs continued in Waffen SS service, albeit in declining numbers, until the end of 1943, many having fought in the great tank battle of Kursk in July. They were slowly replaced by the new Panther tank, which began to enter Waffen SS service during the summer of 1943. Remaining numbers of Panzer IIIs were relegated to second-line formations, although the tank chassis continued to be built for use by other armored vehicles, notably the Sturmgeschütze self-propelled gun.

⚡ Panzer workhorse

The PzKpfw IV had been developed in the late 1930s as a companion tank to the Panzer III. While the Panzer III was intended to spearhead the Blitzkrieg, the Panzer IV was armed with a short-barreled, low-velocity 7.5cm gun to act as a support weapon, destroying enemy strong points with high-explosive shells. This tactical philosophy soon changed with the realization that all battle tanks had to be able to fight other armored vehicles, and this required a long-barreled high-velocity gun.

Below: A PzKpfw III armed with the smaller 3.7cm main gun. These tanks are being made ready for the Nazi invasion of the Soviet Union, June 1941.

Below: A three-quarters view of a PzKpfw IV, armed with a 7.5cm L/48 main gun. The Panzer IV was the only German tank to see continuous service from 1939 to 1945.

PzKpfw IV Tank Ausf J
CREW: Five
WEIGHT: 24.6 tons (25 tonnes)
DIMENSIONS: length (inc. gun) 23ft (7.02m); width 10ft 10in (3.29m); height 8ft 10in (2.68m)
ARMAMENT: 7.5cm KwK 40 L/48 gun; 2 x 7.92mm machine guns (1 co-axial with main gun; 1 in hull front)
ARMOR: turret front 2in (50mm); hull sides 1.2in (30mm); hull rear 0.8in (20mm)
POWERPLANT: 300hp Maybach 12-cylinder petrol engine
PERFORMANCE: max. road speed 24mph (38kph); max. cross-country 15mph (24kph)
RANGE: road 130 miles (210km); cross-country 80 miles (130km)

The Panzer IV was the only German tank that continued in full manufacture from the start to the end of the war, a reflection of its ability to be uprated to meet changing tactical demands. Its gun was steadily improved. Thicker and better-positioned armor was added to the tank, and if the Panzer IV lacked the punch of the later generation of German armored vehicles it still remained a dangerous opponent right up until the surrender in 1945.

Although the Leibstandarte received a few of these short-barreled Panzer IVs, the bulk of the Waffen SS were allocated later designs, the first being the Ausf F2 which had extra armor and a considerably more powerful 7.5cm L/43 gun which could penetrate 3.5in (90mm) of sloped armor at

1100yd (1000m). The Ausf H—the most common model in Waffen SS service—incorporated further improvements, notably a longer L/48 gun. These later models featured extensive use of spaced armor around the turret and Schützen (apron) plates along the side of the tank; they were fitted to counter the use of shaped-charge projectiles by making them detonate on the outer armor, so preventing them from piercing the main armor a few inches away.

Throughout 1944 the Panzer IV helped hold the line on both the Eastern and Western fronts. This was the period when the Waffen SS tank aces began to garner impressive totals of enemy tanks. In the East, the 5th SS Panzer Division 'Wiking' was engaged in the Cherkassy Pocket battle, where

Above: A Waffen SS Panzer IV undergoes roadside maintenance during the Normandy campaign of 1944. German engineers were particularly proficient in getting broken down or damaged vehicles back into service with the minimum delay.

75,000 German troops were surrounded by the Red Army during January–February 1944. The 'Wiking' Division spearheaded the successful breakout, and in the process lost virtually all its armor.

One of the heroes of the breakout was SS-Untersturmführer Kurt Schumacher who was awarded the Knight's Cross when commanding two Panzer IVs. He repeatedly took on superior numbers of Soviet armor and over a period of two days knocked out 21 enemy tanks, an extraordinary figure by any standard.

As the chronic German fuel shortages began to become increasingly acute during 1944, the Panzer IV, which had a relatively frugal consumption, was given a new lease of life. Another factor in the tank's favor was its reliability and general maneuverability, especially in confined spaces. These advantages became apparent during the Ardennes offensive of December 1944. The hilly and narrow lanes were ill-suited to the massive and clumsy Tiger I and Tiger II tanks; as a consequence the Panzer IVs found themselves spearheading the attack with the newer and more powerful tanks in support.

Like the Panzer III, the Panzer IV chassis was also used as the basis for a number of variant armored vehicles, including (with the Panzer III) the Hummel and a series of mounts for mobile anti-aircraft guns. The latter, nicknamed the Möbelwagen (furniture van), were fitted with a 3.7cm anti-aircraft gun; they had previously been towed into action, now the gunners could fire the weapon directly from tank-chassis platform. Although the Panzer III and IV tanks played such a prominent role in various campaigns during World War II, they were always seen by the German Army as a stopgap measure for a new generation of medium and heavy tanks.

⚡ *Emergence of the Panther*

Despite the fact that replacements for the Panzer III and IV had been mooted before the outbreak of war, it was only after the shock of encountering Soviet T-34 medium and KV-1 heavy tanks that serious design work started. The requirement called for a medium tank with a high-velocity gun, thick and well-sloped armor and large road wheels with wide tracks. The first design was a virtual copy of the T-34 but this was rejected in favor of a more advanced design that became the PzKpfw V Panther.

The prototype Panther tank was a considerable

Below: A Panzer IV of the 'Hitlerjugend' Division, equipped with spaced armor around the turret and along the hull sides (Schützen). Spaced armor protected the tank from HEAT projectiles fired by the US Bazooka and the British PIAT.

**PzKpfw V Panther
Tank Ausf G**

CREW: Five

WEIGHT:
44 tons (44.8 tonnes)

DIMENSIONS:
length (inc. gun)
29ft 1in (8.86m);
width 10ft 9in (3.27m);
height 9ft 10in (3m)

ARMAMENT:
7.5cm KwK 42 L/70 gun;
2 x 7.92mm machine
guns (1 co-axial with main
gun; 1 in hull front)

ARMOR:
hull front 3.2in (80mm);
hull sides 1.6in (40mm);
hull rear 1.9in (50mm)

POWERPLANT:
700hp Maybach
V12-cylinder engine

PERFORMANCE:
max. road speed 29mph
(46kph); max. cross-
country 19mph (30kph)

RANGE:
road 124 miles (200km);
cross-country 80 miles
(130km)

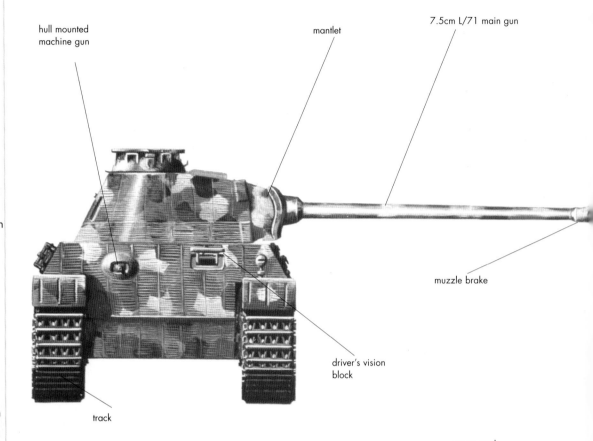

hull mounted
machine gun

mantlet

7.5cm L/71 main gun

muzzle brake

driver's vision
block

track

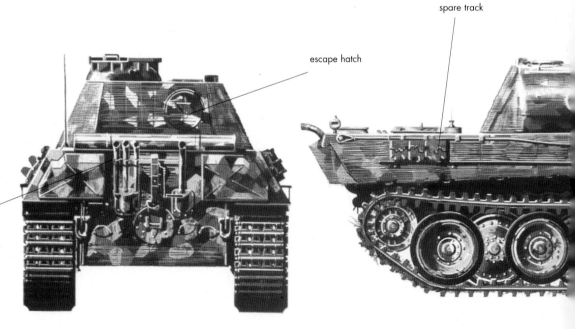

spare track

escape hatch

exhaust from
700bhp
Maybach engine

Above: Once initial teething problems had been overcome the Panther proved itself one of the most formidable armoured fighting vehicles of World War II. Fortunately for the Allies, they were produced in relatively limited numbers.

Left: Three views of a PzKpfw V Panther tank. The well-sloped armor and long-barrelled main armament of the Panther are clearly visible in these illustrations.

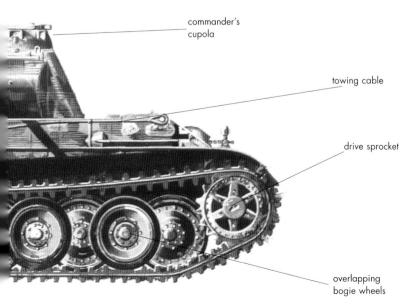

commander's cupola

towing cable

drive sprocket

overlapping bogie wheels

Above: A motorcycle combination passes a Panther tank as part of the 'Hitlerjugend' Division's advance through the streets of Caen in June 1944. The 'Hitlerjugend' played a vital role in holding the Allied advance in the early days of the Normandy landings.

technical advance over its predecessors. It featured the requisite sloping armor, was powered by a 650hp engine, had interleaved wheels with torsion bar suspension and was armed with a 7.5cm L/70 main gun with excellent armor-piercing properties. Unfortunately for the Germans, the tank experienced a series of teething problems, many a consequence of the overrun on weight—the original target of 30 tonnes had risen to 45. Gears and transmission were overstrained and while the engine was powerful enough for the Panther it had a tendency to catch fire through over-heating. Because of Hitler's demand that the tank take part in the battle of Kursk, trials were kept to a minimum and the first

mass production Ausf D Panthers were rushed to the front. Not surprisingly, the Panthers—all in Army service—performed poorly at Kursk, many breaking down before they got into action.

As a result of the Kursk debacle, the Ausf D was discontinued and improvements made to the tank in the form of the Ausf A and then later the Ausf G. Altogether 4800 Panthers were produced. This was considerably less than had been envisaged by its German planners, partly because of the growing problem of Allied air attacks disrupting production, a shortage of raw materials and the complexity of production. While the German small arms industry had learned to simplify its construction methods, tanks and armored vehicles remained slow, expensive and difficult to build.

Despite the restrictions of supply, the Waffen SS had the pick of the selection. This was a far cry from the early years of World War II when they had to live with Army cast-offs and what they could find on the commercial market. By early 1944 each SS panzer division had two tank battalions (each roughly 60 tanks strong), one armed with Panzer IVs the other with the latest Panthers. The one notable exception was the 'Wiking' Division which had both its tank battalions equipped with Panthers.

Despite problems in manufacture and a persistence of technical faults, the late model Panthers were superb tanks. The powerful gun—which had greater penetration than that of the 8.8cm Tiger I— could rip through the heaviest Allied armor, while the Panther's armor made it difficult to knock out in combat, and for a tank of that weight it was fast and reasonably maneuverable.

Besides the main Panther battle tank there were a number of highly successful variants. The Beobachtungspanzer acted as a mobile armored observation post, primarily for forward artillery officers. The Befehlspanzer was a command tank, which (unlike some earlier command vehicles) kept its main armament but carried less ammunition so that a powerful radio could be fitted. The Bergepanzer armored recovery vehicle did away with the turret altogether in favor of a powerful winch and earth anchor to enable recovery of the heaviest tanks (including the Tiger II). The final variant was the Jagdpanther tank destroyer fitted with an 8.8cm L/71 gun.

Below: A Waffen SS Panther prepares for action, Normandy 1944. The high hedgerows of the bocage country of Normandy enabled tanks to be concealed— both from air and ground—and set up possibilities for good ambush positions.

SS *The Tiger tank*

While the Panther may have been one of the best
tanks of the war, the most fearsome was arguably
the PzKpfw VI Tiger I. Planning and design of this
tank took place at a more rapid pace than that of
the Panther: production was started in August 1942
and the Tiger entered service during the winter of
1942–43.

The 55-ton (56-tonnes) Tiger was heavily
armored and equipped with an 8.8cm L/56 main
gun, far superior to anything mounted by the Allies
until well into 1944. The 4-in (100mm) of frontal
armor also ensured that the Tiger was virtually
immune to most other tank guns, so that it could
only be knocked out by well-placed or lucky shot to
the flanks or rear.

On the minus side, the Tiger's weight made the
tank cumbersome in offensive operations and
placed great strain on the transmission and suspension. But a more fundamental weakness lay in

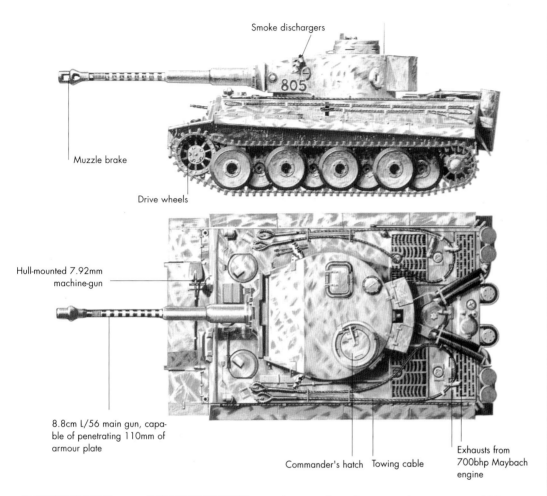

Smoke dischargers

Muzzle brake

Drive wheels

Hull-mounted 7.92mm machine-gun

8.8cm L/56 main gun, capable of penetrating 110mm of armour plate

Commander's hatch   Towing cable

Exhausts from 700bhp Maybach engine

PzKpfw VI Tiger I Tank Ausf E

CREW: Five

WEIGHT:
55.1 tons (55 tonnes)

DIMENSIONS:
length (inc. gun) 27ft (8.34m); width 12ft 3in (3.73m); height 9ft 5in (2.86m)

ARMAMENT:
8.8cm KwK 36 L/56 gun; 2 x 7.92mm machine guns (1 co-axial with main gun; 1 in hull front)

ARMOR:
hull front 3.9in (100mm); hull sides 2.4–3.2in (60–80mm); hull rear 3.2in (80mm)

POWERPLANT:
700hp Maybach V12-cylinder petrol engine

PERFORMANCE:
max. road speed 24mph (38kph); max. cross-country 12.5mph (20kph)

RANGE:
road 62 miles (100km); cross-country 37 miles (60km)

Left: SS-Hauptsturmführer Michael Wittman, the top tank ace of the war. During a career spent fighting on the Eastern Front and in Normandy he knocked out over 130 armored vehicles.

its complicated construction process, which prevented mass production and ensured that relatively few models were manufactured. Whereas the Soviet Union produced approximately 45,000 T-34s during the war, the Germans only built 1350 Tiger Is.

Approximately 500 Tiger tanks were allocated to the Waffen SS, and they were at first deployed in three divisional heavy tank companies—one each for the Leibstandarte, 'Das Reich' and 'Totenkopf' panzer divisions—and then as three independent tank battalions operating at corps level. A few Tiger tanks were used in action by the SS during the recapture of Kharkov in February–March 1943, and they spearheaded the German assault against the Soviet defensive lines on the Kursk salient in July 1943, where they repeatedly proved their worth in

tank-versus-tank operations. In one extraordinary engagement during the Kursk battle, a solitary Tiger of the Leibstandarte engaged a formation of around 50 T-34s, knocking out 22 of them and forcing the remainder to retreat in disarray.

During the Normandy campaign of the summer of 1944, the Waffen SS Tigers were again in the thick of the action. The close terrain and defensive nature of the fighting suited the Tiger I and the Waffen SS tankmen, whose superior tactical skill ensured that they caused disproportionately heavy casualties against the Allies.

Of the many Waffen SS tank aces, the most successful was SS-Hauptsturmführer Michael Wittman. He first saw combat in Poland and Western Europe. At the outbreak of the Russian

Above: *Allied air superiority in the West forced German armoured formations to restrict their daylight movement to a minimum and to adopt strict camouflage discipline. Here, a Waffen SS Tiger tank is carefully camouflaged with local vegetation.*

Right: *A Panzer IV (left) passes a Tiger tank (right). The Tiger's wide tracks—designed to aid movement over snow and mud—are evident when compared with those of the Panzer IV.*

Above: A Tiger of the 1st SS Panzer Corps. The Corps' insignia—a skeleton key within a shield, plus oak leaves —is clearly visible on the hull front.

invasion, he gained instant recognition with the 14th Corps after knocking out six tanks out of an eight-tank entourage in a skirmish in the south sector of the front line.

By November of 1941, he had received the Iron Cross, Second Class, the Wound Badge and the Close Combat Badge. Serving on the Eastern Front he had amassed a score of 117 enemy vehicles destroyed by early 1944. In January 1944, Wittman led his Panzer unit in an amazing battle that halted an entire Soviet tank brigade. For this he received the Knight's Cross, then shortly afterwards, the Oakleaves to this award.

In the summer of 1944 Michael Wittman's unit was deployed in the defense of Normandy. It was there that he scored his greatest single combat success. Wittman's company of 13 tanks caught a tank column from the British 7th Armored Division by surprise in and around the village of Villers-Bocage.

Playing a leading role in the operation, Wittman

Right: A Tiger I advances across farmland, Northern France, 1944. The Tiger I earned a uniquely fearful reputation amongst American and British soldiers.

Below: A Waffen SS Tiger II is made ready for action in the streets of the Hungarian capital of Budapest during the latter stages of the war.

destroyed the lead and rear tanks and then ran along the trapped column shooting up the remaining armored vehicles in turn. In the whole engagement, 47 Allied vehicles were destroyed for the loss of just four Tigers. SS-Hauptsturmführer Michael Wittman's luck was not to last as he and his crew were killed in a battle with Canadian armor on August 8.

SS *The King Tiger*

Once the Panther and Tiger were in production, German tank designers became obsessed with increasing the offensive and defensive powers of their armored vehicles—at the expense of mobility and reliability. During September 1944 production of the Tiger I tank ended, to be superseded by an even

Above: A unit of Waffen SS Tiger IIs is inspected by its commanding officer. The sheer bulk of these tanks can be seen in this photograph.

heavier and more powerful tank: the PzKpfw VI Tiger II Ausf B (colloquially known as the Königstiger, or King Tiger).

During 1943 the arms manufacturers Henschel and Porsche were asked to provide designs for the new tank. Henschel eventually won the design competition, although the first 50 Tiger IIs were fitted with the Porsche turrets. Thereafter all other tanks conformed to the Henschel design; just under 500 tanks were constructed before the Henschel factory was overrun by the Allies in 1945.

The Tiger II incorporated aspects of the Tiger I and the Panther (a Panther II had been envisaged but did not see the light of day, in part because of the decision to proceed with the Tiger II). The armor was extremely thick, reaching 7.3in (185mm) on the turret face, and in common with the Panther it was well sloped to deflect enemy shot. The long-barreled 8.8cm L/71 was the best armor-piercing gun fielded in any German tank of the war.

The increase in armor protection for the tank had an obvious consequence: an increase in weight. At

nearly 70 tons, the Tiger II was an ungainly monster. It used much the same 700hp engine installed in later model Panthers, which meant that the Tiger II (along with the Tiger I) was under-powered for its size. It also had an enormous thirst for fuel, and at a time when fuel shortages were biting deeply into what remained of the German economy, a tank with such poor fuel economy and limited range was something of a liability.

During periods of mobile warfare, particularly when the Germans were being forced to retreat, Tiger IIs regularly ran out of fuel and had to be abandoned. And in certain types of offensive action, such as the attack through the Ardennes in December 1944, the Tiger II lacked sufficient mobility for the operation and had to be held in reserve. But in static, defensive warfare the Tiger IIs could be quite devastating, acting as strong points in the German line, able to destroy enemy armor out to ranges of 3500yd (3200m) while being virtually invulnerable to enemy counter-fire.

The Tiger IIs of the Waffen SS were distributed in heavy tank battalions, which initially served at corps level although by the end of 1944 were reassigned to army level—although by that time the grand SS armies envisaged by Hitler and Himmler were little more than paper concoctions. Tiger IIs fought with some distinction in the final battles on the Eastern Front, but were too few to have any effect on the conduct of operations. While the German forces undoubtedly possessed the most powerful tanks on the battlefield, they lacked the fuel, numbers and mobility of their Allied counterparts—and in the end that was what counted most.

Left: Carrying a squad of paratroopers, a Tiger II of the Waffen SS advances during the abortive Ardennes offensive of 1944–45. The paratrooper on the left is armed with an StG 44 assault rifle, while the soldier on the right carries a Soviet PPSh sub-machine gun.

PzKpfw VI Tiger II Tank

CREW: Five

WEIGHT(WITH HENSCHEL TURRET): 68.3 tons (69.4 tonnes)

DIMENSIONS: length (inc. gun) 33ft 8in (10.26m); width 12ft 4in (3.75m); height 10ft 2in (3.1m)

ARMAMENT: 8.8cm KwK 43 L/71 gun; 2 x 7.92mm machine guns (1 co-axial with main gun; 1 in hull front)

ARMOR: hull front 5.9in (150mm); hull sides 3.2in (80mm); hull rear 3.2in (80mm)

POWERPLANT: 700hp Maybach 12-cylinder petrol engine

PERFORMANCE: max. road speed 24mph (38kph); max. cross-country 11mph (17km/h)

RANGE: road 68 miles (110km); cross-country 53 miles (85km)

8 Assault Guns and Tank Destroyers

The tank was not the only Waffen SS armored fighting vehicle. During the war a series of vehicles— some quickly improvised, others carefully planned —entered service to supplement the tank.

Above: *A Sturmgeschütz III advances over a culvert in Italy during a bombardment of Allied positions.*

SS Assault guns

Within the panzer division there was a tendency for the tanks to leave the infantry and artillery behind as they surged forward to exploit the breakthrough in the enemy's line. As a consequence, there was a call by both infantry and artillery for an armored close-support vehicle to knock out bunkers and other enemy strong points. This vehicle would be highly mobile and also have sufficient protection to operate in a front-line environment, unlike conventional artillery. The answer to this demand was the assault gun, or Sturmgeschütz. The first of these armored fighting vehicles was delivered to the

German armed forces in 1940 and was designated the Sturmgeschütz (StuG) III.

The StuG III used the chassis of the Panzer III (hence its III designation) but dispensed with a turret, and, instead, a 7.5cm gun was installed directly into the superstructure. Better armored than most German tanks of the time, with a low silhouette, the StuG III proved a valuable support weapon. And it was also easier and cheaper to build than a standard tank. Ammunition included high-explosive, smoke and armor-piercing, although its low velocity L/24 gun—the same as that used in the early Panzer IV—was unsuited to anti-tank operations. The 1940 campaign in the West convinced the German authorities of the need for an anti-tank requirement, and

over the next couple of years the gun of the StuG III was replaced by progressively longer models, initially the L/43 and then the L/48.

This emphasis on an anti-tank capability began to change the role of the StuG III from a true assault gun to that of a panzerjaeger (tank hunter/destroyer). And as the panzer divisions were always short of tanks, so the StuG III was used to reinforce the tank battalions. Although the StuG III proved effective in this role—a tank on the cheap—it took it away from the infantry who now lacked that useful close fire-support. This shortcoming was eventually rectified with the emergence of a range of weapon-carrying half-tracks which operated closely with the ground troops.

StuG III Assault Gun Ausf G

CREW: Four

WEIGHT:
23.5 tons (23.9 tonnes)

DIMENSIONS:
length (inc. gun) 22ft 3in (6.78m); width 9ft 8in (2.95m); height 7ft 1in (2.16m)

ARMAMENT:
7.5cm KwK 40 L/48 gun; possibly 1 x 7.92mm machine gun on roof

ARMOR:
hull front 2in (50mm); hull sides 1.2in (30mm); hull rear 1.2in (30mm)

POWERPLANT:
300hp Maybach V12-cylinder petrol engine

PERFORMANCE:
max. road speed 28mph (45kph); max. cross-country 12mph (19kph)

RANGE:
road 100 miles (161km); cross-country 60 miles (97km)

Left: *A StuG III passes a line of weary infantry. Armed with an L/48 main gun, this StuG III would be primarily employed in a tank-hunting role.*

Below: An officer and NCO of the 'Wiking' Division stand in front of their Marder II, during the Eastern Front summer offensive of July 1942. Spare track is attached to the Marder's hull to provide additional protection.

The StuG III was, in fact, the first armored fighting vehicle to be allotted to the Waffen SS, with vehicles arriving during the summer of 1940. In the period before the invasion of the Soviet Union in June 1941, the Leibstandarte, 'Reich' and 'Totenkopf' all received batteries of the StuG III. By early 1943 the batteries had been expanded into battalions, each deploying 21 assault guns. Because they were relatively easy to manufacture and had proved themselves in a combat role, production of the StuG III continued to the end of the war, making it the most common armored vehicle in Waffen SS service.

SS *The Marder*

As the Germans pressed deeper into the Soviet Union in 1941–42, so the need for mobile anti-tank guns to counter the Red Army's vast tank arsenal became ever more apparent. As a stopgap measure, the Marder (marten) series of light tank destroyers was introduced in the summer of 1942. The Marder II was a straightforward combination of a Panzer II chassis and a 7.5cm Pak 40 anti-tank gun (although originally it had been planned to use a 5cm gun). In contrast to the StuG III, crew protection was rudimentary, consisting of a simple three-sided shield,

Left: A Marder III advances across the Russian steppe. Maneuverable and cheap to manufacture, the Marder series proved very effective as a stop-gap tank destroyer.

Marder III Tank Destroyer Ausf M

CREW: Four

WEIGHT:
10.8 tons (11 tonnes)

DIMENSIONS:
length (inc. gun) 15ft 3in
(4.65m); width 7ft 9in
(2.35m); height 8ft 2in
(2.48m)

ARMAMENT:
7.5cm Pak 40/3 gun

ARMOR:
hull front 0.8in (20mm);
hull sides 0.6in (15mm);
hull rear 0.3in (8mm)

POWERPLANT:
150hp Praga petrol
engine

PERFORMANCE:
max. road speed 26mph
(42kph); max. cross-
country 15mph (24kph)

RANGE:
road 115 miles (185km);
cross-country 87 miles
(140km)

---

mounted high on the superstructure.

Although far from being at the cutting edge of German panzer technology, the Marder II proved an effective tank hunter: its 7.5cm gun was sufficiently powerful to knock out all but the heaviest Soviet tanks (which only began to appear from 1944 onward), and its relatively small size and general cross-country mobility made it popular with its crews. And, more to the point, there was a surplus of Panzer II chassises and the Marder was a cheap and easy conversion. Over 1200 Marder IIs were manufactured and substantial numbers saw service with the Leibstandarte, 'Das Reich', 'Totenkopf' and 'Wiking' divisions on the Eastern Front.

The Marder III was developed along the same

lines and at the same time as the Marder II, but used the Czech-designed Panzer 38(t) to provide the chassis. Again, a simple three-sided shield was employed to protect the crew, although the main armament fitted on the earlier models was the captured Soviet 76.2mm field gun, which gave good service as an anti-tank weapon. Subsequently, when more 7.5cm Pak 40s became available, the Soviet gun was replaced by the German one. A third change that took place on later Marder IIIs consisted of a reconfiguration of the whole vehicle: the engine was moved to the front and the fighting platform moved back to the rear of the chassis. This gave the vehicle much better balance and improved maneuverability.

During 1942–43, the Marder IIs and IIIs were

among the few armored vehicles that deployed a sufficiently powerful gun to deal with the Soviet armor of the period. And it was only when a new generation of tank hunters began to appear in 1944 that the Marder took a more subsidiary role.

⚡ The Hetzer

While the Marders had been fairly hasty improvisations, the Hetzer (baiter—as in bear-baiting) was specifically designed as a lightweight tank hunter. The Germans were slow in getting the project off the ground, however; design work only began in 1943 and the first production models were not ready until the following year.

The versatile Panzer 38(t) provided the Hetzer with its chassis. The Hetzer's superstructure consisted of a well-sloped armor-plate carapace—up to 2.4in (60mm) thick—in which was mounted a 7.5cm anti-tank gun.

Its low-silhouette and good cross-country mobility made the Hetzer an immediate success with anti-tank battalions and demand was strong. Although able to knock out most enemy armor, the Hetzer's popularity was mainly due to the fact that this small vehicle was hard to hit, survivability being a major factor in all armored crews' appreciation of a particular vehicle or weapon.

An advanced feature of the Hetzer was the 7.92mm machine gun mounted on the hull top. This was operated by remote control by the commander within the vehicle.

⚡ The Jagdpanzer IV Series

Experience on the Eastern Front in 1942 convinced the German Army that the StuG III would need a more powerful gun if it was to operate effectively in its tank-hunter role. Rather than modify the already

Left: Another innovative use of the Czech 38(t) chassis—the Hetzer tank destroyer. Important advantages for this vehicle included a low profile and well-sloped armor.

Hetzer Tank Destroyer

CREW: Four

WEIGHT:
14.3 tons (14.5 tonnes)

DIMENSIONS:
length (inc. gun) 20ft 4in (6.2m); width 8ft 2in (2.5m); height 6ft 11in (2.1m)

ARMAMENT:
7.5cm Pak 39 gun; 1 x 7.92mm machine gun (roof mounted)

ARMOR:
hull front 2.4in (60mm); hull sides 0.8in (20mm); hull rear 0.3in (8mm)

POWERPLANT:
160hp Praga petrol engine

PERFORMANCE:
max. road speed 24mph (39kph); max. cross-country 15mph (24kph)

RANGE:
road 155 miles (250km); cross-country 50 miles (80km)

cramped Panzer III chassis, which underpinned the StuG III, it was decided to use the Panzer IV chassis and provide it with the long-barreled 7.5cm L/70 gun designed for the Panther tank.

Production problems in fitting the L/70 gun into the new tank destroyer led to an interim solution of going back to the 7.5cm L/48 gun used in the StuG III. This compromise vehicle was designated the Sturmgeschütz (StuG) IV. With its low height, good armor protection, and provision of two machine guns the new tank destoryer was held in high regard by German anti-tank crews. The 'Hitlerjugend' Division was the first Waffen SS formation to receive the StuG IV during the spring of 1944, and during the rest of the year more went to the other panzer and panzer-grenadier divisions.

Towards the end of 1944 the L/70 armed Jagdpanzer IV finally entered service with the Waffen SS, and was called the Panzer IV/70 (V). The new gun certainly gave the tank destroyer and extra edge in terms of armor penetration, but its long barrel made it nose-heavy and caused extra wear on the forward road wheels.

A further variant simplified the conversion process and was designated the Panzer IV/70(A). During 1944 the various Jagdpanzer IVs replaced the Marders as the main tank-hunting strike force.

◪ The Jagdpanther

The famous Jagdpanzer V Jagdpanther was a tank hunter that had it been built in sufficient numbers could have made a decisive intervention on the bat-tlefield. Of all the tank hunters deployed by the Germans this was their finest weapon. Although obviously based on the Panther tank, the conver-sion was carefully thought out and featured a thick and well-sloped armored hull which helped deflect enemy AP shot. Its overall shape made it perfect for adopting hull-down defensive positions, so that

Right: Lines of German assault guns—including StuG IVs—are displayed by their Soviet captors in the Crimea, 1944. By this stage of the war such losses of vital armor were irreplaceable.

only the main armament and a small portion of the upper superstructure was visible to the enemy. And for a vehicle weighing in at around 45 tons it was remarkably mobile, its 700hp engine providing a swift maximum road speed of 34mph (55kph), while its cross-country performance was compared favorably by its crews to other tank destroyers.

The Jagdpanther was armed with the same 8.8cm Pak 43 L/71 gun used by the Tiger II. This gun could eliminate virtually all tanks at ranges of up to 2750yd (2500m), and for the very heaviest Soviet armor—such as the huge JS III with frontal armor as thick as 9in (230mm) in places—the Panzergranate 40/43 AP round could penetrate 10.8in (275mm) of

armor plate at 575yd (500m). Secondary armament included a hull-mounted machine gun and a rather curious device situated on the roof, which projected an explosive charge around the vehicle if it came under attack by enemy infantry.

Fortunately for the Allies, less than 400 Jagdpanthers were built, with limited numbers being issued to the Waffen SS. In the failed attempt to raise the siege of Budapest in January 1945, 'Das Reich', 'Hohenstaufen', and 'Frundsberg' each deployed a company of Jagdpanthers, totaling 42 vehicles. During the following months the numbers of Jagdpanthers were steadily whittled down to just six vehicles by April 10, in the aftermath of the

German retreat from Vienna.

The story of Germany's assault guns and tank destroyers illustrates the strengths and weaknesses of the German arms industry as a whole. The Germans were highly imaginative in the way they gave old or even obsolete tanks a new lease of life by converting them into self-propelled guns of one sort or another. The German arms industry, however, chose too many options and configurations and their construction techniques owed too much to craft industries and too little to mass production. Although the United States and the Soviet Union never managed to produce armored fighting vehicles to match the best the Germans had to offer, they manufactured a smaller range of vehicles but at a far greater rate. Ultimately, German armor was overwhelmed by the numerical superiority of the Allied forces.

Below: The commander of a Jagdpanther surveys the battlefield. Although much photographed for propaganda purposes, relatively few of these formidable fighting vehicles were manufactured by Nazi Germany.

Jagdpanther Tank Destroyer

CREW: Four

WEIGHT:
45.3 tons (46 tonnes)

DIMENSIONS:
length (inc. gun) 32ft 6in (9.90m); width 10ft 9in (3.27m); height 8ft 11in (2.72m)

ARMAMENT:
8.8cm Pak 43/3 L/71 gun; 1 x 7.92mm machine gun (in hull front)

ARMOR:
hull front 3.2in (80mm); hull sides 1.6in (40mm); hull rear 1.6in (40mm)

POWERPLANT:
700hp Maybach V12-cylinder petrol engine

PERFORMANCE:
max. road speed 34mph (55kph); max. cross-country 15mph (24kph)

RANGE:
road 130 miles (210km); cross-country 87 miles (140km)

9 *Support Vehicles*

The Waffen SS divisions used an array of half-tracks, armored cars, trucks, and motorcycles during the course of the war.

Above: The flame-thrower version of the SdKfz 251 in action, one of the most versatile of German half-track vehicles.

The tanks and self-propelled guns of a Waffen SS panzer division understandably took most of the limelight but they formed only a small percentage of the vehicles deployed within the division. In the spring of 1944 the 2nd SS Panzer Division 'Das Reich' had an establishment strength of 126 tanks in two tank battalions and some 92 self-propelled guns of differing types, and yet their were at least 3000 vehicles within the division, ranging from half-tracks and armored cars to trucks, cars (military and civilian) and motorcycles.

⚡ *Half-tracks*

Half-tracks—driven by caterpillar tracks with conventional front wheels for steering—became the workhorses of the panzer division, transporting infantry, artillery and combat engineers into the heart of the battle. Over the course of the war a multitude of half-tracks saw service, but most were of two types: the armored personal carrier (APC) and the artillery tractor, the latter designed to tow artillery pieces while having sufficient space to carry their crew.

In the 1930s, when the panzer division was being thought out, the Army Weapons Department called for a light and a medium APC to carry panzer grenadiers to the battlefield and provide them with a degree of protection in the process. Once in the front line, the panzer grenadiers would jump out of the vehicles and fight on foot.

The light APC requirement became the Sonderkraftwagen (SdKfz) 250, which first saw action in 1940. The SdKfz 250 could hold a crew of five men plus the driver, who were contained within a lightly armored open-topped hull—with a typical armament of one or two machine guns.

As the SdKfz 250 could not take a full infantry squad, it tended to perform roles such as mobile command/communications post and, increasingly, weapons carrier; among the latter were the 250/7 (8.1cm mortar), 250/8 (7.5cm L/24 assault gun), 250/9 (2cm anti-aircraft gun) and 250/10 (3.7cm anti-tank gun). The SdKfz 250 provided otherwise vulnerable ground troops with a greater degree of self-protection.

The SdKfz 251 was essentially an extended version of the SdKfz 250, and could transport an

Below: An SdKfz 10 transports Waffen SS infantry in Normandy during the Allied invasion of 1944. A somewhat half-hearted attempt has been made to camouflage the vehicle from Allied aircraft.

SdKfz 251/1 Half-Track

CREW: 11, plus driver

WEIGHT:
7.69 tons (7.81 tonnes)

DIMENSIONS:
length 19ft 3in (5.8m);
width 6ft 11in (2.1m);
height 5ft 9in (1.75m)

ARMAMENT:
1/2 x 7.92mm
machine guns

POWERPLANT:
100hp Maybach 6-
cylinder petrol engine

PERFORMANCE:
max. road speed 33mph
(53kph); max. cross-
country 18mph (29kph)

RANGE:
road 186 miles (300km);
cross-country 80 miles
(130km)

infantry squad of 11 men (plus driver). As a result it became one of the most ubiquitous battlefield vehicles within the panzer division—some 16,000 SdKfz 251 half-tracks were built between 1939 and 1945. Once early mechanical problems were resolved, the SdKfz 251 was regarded by the troops as a dependable and effective 'battle taxi', although this APC's greatest claim to fame lay in its versatility—some 22 variants were produced during its production lifetime. While the straightforward APC was the most common variant, the SdKfz 251 (like its sister half-track SdKfz250) increasingly began to take on the role as weapons carrier, which besides mortars, assault guns, light anti-aircraft and anti-tank guns, included sound and flash-spotting vehicles for the artillery and a flamethrower.

As more weapons were added to the half-track, so its tactical role changed. Instead of acting as a simple APC that dropped-off its crew at the battle start line and then retired to relative safety, the weapons-carrying half-track now found itself an integral part of the battle. While providing valuable fire-power to the infantry, open-topped half-tracks were lightly armored—0.6in (14mm) maximum—and vulnerable to artillery fire anti-tank weapons. Rising casualties were an inevitable consequence.

Waffen SS formations only began to acquire APC half-tracks from 1942 onward, when they progressively converted to panzer grenadier and then full panzer divisions. At first, only one of the division's panzer-grenadier (infantry) battalion was fully equipped with half-tracks. Over time, however, priority in weapon allocation ensured that a Waffen SS panzer division could deploy anything up 300 of these vehicles.

The German Army fielded several different types of artillery tractor half-track, each intended for carrying particular loads, and included the medium SdKfz 7 and the light SdKfz 10. The SdKfz 7 towed the division's heavier artillery, including the 8.8cm Flak gun and the 10.5cm and 15cm howitzers. This half-track was also able to carry 12 men—sitting in bench seats behind the driver—plus extra stores and ammunition. The insatiable demand for mobile

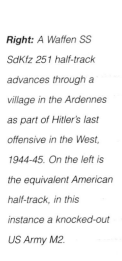

Right: A Waffen SS SdKfz 251 half-track advances through a village in the Ardennes as part of Hitler's last offensive in the West, 1944-45. On the left is the equivalent American half-track, in this instance a knocked-out US Army M2.

weapon platforms extended to this vehicle as well, and conversions included the SdKfz 7/1, mounting a 2cm Flakvierling 38 quad anti-aircraft gun, and the SdKfz 7/2 with a single 3.7cm AA gun.

The most common of the half-track artillery tractors was the SdKfz 10, 17,000 of them being built before 1945. This lightweight vehicle was used to transport infantry weapons and light artillery. Using the same chassis as the SdKfz 250, it was a highly successful half-track and with all such vehicles demand was greater than supply. The dominance of Allied air power, especially in the West, led to several SdKfz 10 half-tracks to be converted to AA gun platforms with single-barreled 2cm guns.

SS *Armored Cars*

Germany was a pioneer of armored-car development, and in the early 1930s had produced the six-wheeled heavy SdKfz 231. Armed with a 2cm gun and 7.92mm machine gun this early design was based on a commercial truck chassis and engine, but it lacked the strength and power for its chosen

Above: SS soldiers stand by a radio-fitted Kübelwagen, the German version of the Allied 'jeep'. A total of 17,000 of these highly useful command and reconnaissance vehicles were built during the war.

role. Although production ceased in 1935, the six-wheeled SdKfz 231 saw active service during the early stages of the war. Its replacement was the

Kübelwagen

WEIGHT:
1400lb (635kg)

DIMENSIONS:
length 12ft 3in (3.73m);
width 5ft 3in (1.60m);
height 4ft 5in (1.35m)

POWERPLANT:
24hp Volkswagen 4-cylinder petrol engine

Left: A 'Hitlerjugend' Kübelwagen—in its amphibious Schwimmwagen version —motors through a village in Normandy, June-July 1944. The propeller for amphibious operations can be seen at the rear of the vehicle.

Above: Driving a Schwimmwagen, SS troops of the Leibstandarte pause by the roadside during the Ardennes offensive.

eight-wheeled SdKfz 231 (8-rad)—the 8-rad (wheel) suffix being appended to avoid confusion. Powered by a 150hp engine the SdKfz 231 (8-rad) was better suited to operations in the field than the 80hp six-wheeled version. The series also included the usual command vehicle, with extra radio equipment, and the SdKfz 233 which mounted a short-barreled 7.5cm L/24 assault gun.

In 1935 the Army acquired a light armored car, the SdKfz 221, which after some development work evolved into the SdKfz 222. This small and maneuverable vehicle proved popular with reconnaissance troops. Within a small open-topped turret was a 2cm gun and a 7.92m machine gun—substantial armament for so small a vehicle.

The Waffen SS were slow to receive armored

cars, and it was only after the they were uprated to panzer-grenadier divisions did they get an adequate allocation. After the invasion of the Soviet Union the Army and Waffen SS began to ask for more powerful vehicles with a heavier armament. As a result, the older Sdkz 231 (8-rad) and SdKfz 222 were reassigned to anti-partisan duties, predominantly in the Balkans, while a second generation of armored cars began to enter front-line service.

The eight-wheeled SdKfz 234 series was better armed and armored than its predecessors. The SdKfz 234/1 was the command vehicle, armed with just a 2cm gun. The SdKfz 234/2 Puma, one of the best armored cars of the war, was fitted with an enclosed turret with a 5cm anti-tank gun and co-axial machine gun. The 210hp engine was able to provide adequate power to the Puma, providing it with a maximum road speed of 53mph (85 kmh). From late 1943 onward the reconnaissance battalions of the Waffen SS panzer divisions began to receive the Puma. Two further SdKfz 234 variants were armed with 7.5cm guns but the Puma remained the better all-round vehicle.

SS *Light vehicles*

During the 1930s the German logistical department attempted to standardize the profusion of trucks within the military system—over 100 in 1939—in their Einheit (standard) program. The new system did not last long, however, and collapsed during the

course of the war when the German armed forces requisitioned trucks and cars (both military and civilian) from the many nations they had overrun in 1939–41. By the time of the invasion of the Soviet Union in June 1941 there were an astounding 1500 different types of vehicle being used by the Germans—a logistical nightmare.

Later in the war, the Schell program attempted to bring some form of order to this chaotic situation but the problem was never resolved. Among this plethora of vehicles, a few stand out. The most successful German Army truck was the Opel Blitz, and some 25,000 of these four-wheel drive medium trucks were built. The Opel Blitz trucks were employed in a wide variety of roles besides general

Below: Wearing a distinctive fez, the Brigadeführer of the 23rd Waffen Gebirgs Division der SS 'Kama' climbs aboard a Schwimmwagen.

Top: *Wearing an Italian-pattern camouflage tunic, the commander of the 'Hitlerjugend' panzer regiment rides a motorcycle combination, Normandy 1944.*

supply, including fulfilling duties as a field ambulance, mobile workshop, command post, mobile laundry and radio van.

The Volkswagen Kübel (bucket) achieved near legendary status as the German 'jeep', 55,000 being produced in a run lasting between 1940 and 1944. The origins of the Kübelwagen lay in the much-touted 'people's car' (Volkswagen) of the 1930s, whose

production was hijacked by the Army to become the Kübelwagen. Simple to build and rugged enough to survive the conditions encountered on the Eastern Front, the Kübelwagen proved a great success as a small command vehicle.

The lightest vehicles used by the Wehrmacht and Waffen SS were motorcycles, employed singly or with a sidecar. The reconnaissance battalion used them extensively for scouting duties, while in the division as a whole they were invaluable for dispatch riders. Army officers also found them useful as a means of getting past the massive traffic jams that became an integral part of a panzer division on the move.

Of the many civilian motorcycles adapted by the German military system, many were supplied by BMW and Zündap. When used in motorcycle combination form, an MG 34 machine gun was often mounted on the sidecar, thereby providing the motorcycle team with a sharp bite if it came into contact with the enemy.

Right: A motorcycle combination of the Leibstandarte advances through a burning town during the Polish campaign of September 1939. The unit insignia painted on the sidecar is a skeleton key (Dietrich), a pun on the name of the Leibstandarte's infamous commander, Sepp Dietrich.

Left: Totally exhausted by their endeavours, the crew of a motorcycle combination rests during the epic defense of Caan by the Waffen SS, Normandy 1944.

10 Uniforms and Insignia

The Waffen SS, in fact, became a pioneer in the development of military uniforms—and its ideas were to have a lasting influence in the postwar world.

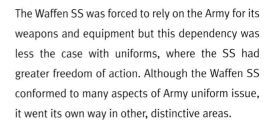

Right: A tunic and cap of the Stosstrupp Adolf Hitler in 1923—an early forerunner of the Waffen SS. The tunic is the Reichsheer pattern, the cap Austrian in origin.

The Waffen SS was forced to rely on the Army for its weapons and equipment but this dependency was less the case with uniforms, where the SS had greater freedom of action. Although the Waffen SS conformed to many aspects of Army uniform issue, it went its own way in other, distinctive areas.

In the introduction of camouflage and cold-weather clothing the Waffen SS achieved notable firsts. In this respect, the Waffen SS saw itself as a revolutionary new institution, which, unlike the 'reactionary' Army, was eager to embrace new ideas and attitudes, whether in training, tactics or uniforms. But at the same time—reflecting, in particular, the influence and ideas of its leader, Reichsführer SS Heinrich Himmler—the SS drew inspiration from Germany's past.

The black uniform, one of the defining elements of the SS's visual projection of itself, was derived from a number of sources: the black-uniformed Prussian guard hussars dating back to before Frederick the Great's time, the German Freikorps who operated on the Eastern Front at the end of World War I and Mussolini's black-shirted fascists. And the most infamous item of Waffen SS insignia—the Totenkopf or death's head—had similar precedents, both historical and contemporary. As well as their

Left: *SS officer Julius Schreck, photographed in 1933. Complementing his black uniform is an early example of the 'crusher' cap, where the wire lining has been removed from the cap to give it its distinctive appearance. The death's head symbol became an important—although not exclusive—symbol of the SS.*

Right: A full-dress
greatcoat of the
Leibstandarte
'Adolf Hitler', worn
on ceremonial
occasions during the
prewar period.

black uniforms, the Prussian guard hussars also adopted the Totenkopf emblem after the death of Frederick William I in 1740, as did other German units down the centuries. During World War I, German storm troops used the emblem, to be followed by Freikorps members immediately after the war. And in the 1930s the Army's panzer troops adopted the skull and crossbones as their distinguishing badge of service.

While the black uniforms and Totenkopf had a long history in Germany, these symbols of darkness and death perfectly suited the violent and ruthless philosophy of the SS. Himmler—forever looking back to Germany's mythical past—also encouraged interest in Germanic runes and this led to the adoption of the two 'lightning-flash' sig-runes worn on the SS soldier's collar. A sign of victory, the sig-runes became another means to distinguish the Waffen SS from the Army, and in the eyes of Hitler and Himmler these symbols helped set it apart as a political and military elite.

A further symbol used to emphasize the elite nature of the Waffen SS was the ceremonial dagger, issued to all qualified SS men. Although there were a number of specially commissioned daggers, the two main types comprised the 1933 and 1936 patterns. The 1933 pattern was inscribed with the individual's SS number and carried the SS motto: Meine Ehre Heisst Treue ('Loyalty is my Honor'). The 1936 pattern was slightly simplified, dispensing with the SS number, and this made it more appropriate for the mass production that became necessary with the wartime expansion of the Waffen SS. Nonetheless, both patterns were made to a high specification and used quality materials. Each SS man was expected to look after his dagger—usually only worn on ceremonial occasions—with the greatest of care. As it was considered a badge of office, to lose or otherwise dispose of the dagger was a disciplinary offense.

Left: *This example of the black service uniform is being worn by Heinrich Schmauser, Führer of the SS Oberabschnitt Süd, 1935. The award of the Iron Cross First Class iis attached to his left breast pocket.*

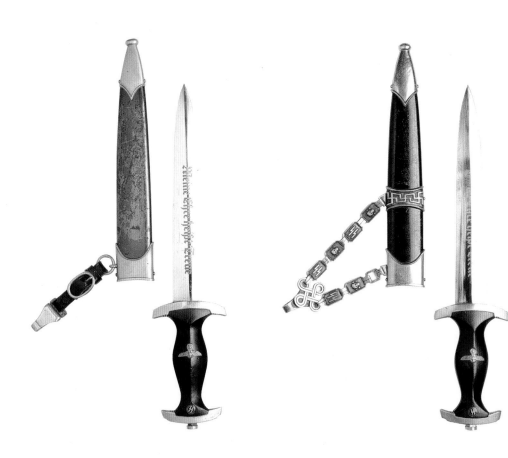

Right: The two patterns of ceremonial dagger that played such a key part in SS ritual—the 1933 pattern (left) and the 1936 pattern.

Prewar and Ceremonial Uniforms

The black uniform, formalized in 1932, followed the lifting on the ban on political uniforms by the Weimar government. The black uniform was worn on pre-war ceremonial occasions and, sometimes during the war, by Waffen SS officers on leave. The Allgemeine SS (general SS, or those members of the SS not in other branches of the organization) continued to wear the black uniform, but after the declaration of war in 1939 it was worn less frequently.

During the 1930s the SS expanded its range of ceremonial and full-dress uniforms, with the Leibstandarte SS 'Adolf Hitler' taking the lead in this field. In the summer months, for example,

Leibstandarte officers could wear a white full-dress uniform. But this situation changed with the advent of war in 1939; Waffen SS ceremonial uniforms were packed away and by the time of the invasion of the Soviet Union in 1941 they were fast becoming a distant memory.

Headgear

In the pre-war period many Waffen SS troops still wore the ungainly 1916/18 steel helmets, although by the outbreak of war the majority of troops were equipped with the standard 1935-pattern helmet. In 1935, individual unit insignias were replaced by a standardized design: black SS runes on a silver shield on the right-side of the helmet; a red shield

Left: The summer ceremonial uniform of a Sturmbannführer of the Leibstandarte 'Adolf Hitler', 1939–40.

Above: *The standard 1942-pattern helmet with the SS-runes shield*

Above: *The field cap of an SS general officer with aluminum piping and insignia of zinc alloy. The SS version of the Wehrmacht eagle is positioned above the death's head insignia.*

Below: *Otto Kumm in the uniform of an SS Standartenführer (an equivalent rank to colonel) with the prestigious award of the Knight's Cross at his neck. Kumm commanded a standarte of the 'Das Reich' Division at the Battle of Kharkov (1943) and went on to command the 'Prinz Eugen' Division.*

within which was a white disc containing a black swastika on the left side (although in 1940 this was removed for camouflage reasons).

Polizei units continued to wear their own individual insignia which included the police badge worn on the left side of the helmet. The only further change in the steel helmet was the issue of the 1942-pattern; it was cheaper to manufacture but apart from a slightly sharper outline differed little from the previous pattern.

The original officer's peaked cap (Schirmmütze) —black with white piping, aluminum chin strap cords and Totenkopf badge—was replaced in the late 1930s by a field-gray cap with a black band and black leather peak. NCOs wore a similar cap with a gray cloth peak. The NCO cap was also manufactured without the aluminum cords and internal stiffener, allowing it to be easily folded away when not being worn. Nicknamed the 'crusher', this cap became highly popular with front-line soldiers, and with many officers who took out the stiffener from their own caps.

The 1934 field cap (Feldmütze) was similar to the Army pattern, and its fore-and-aft shape gained it the nickname of Schiffchen or 'little ship', and while not a particularly useful item of headgear it was worn throughout the war by other ranks, NCOs and officers. In 1943 a more practical form of headgear was introduced, the Einheitsfeldmütze, which was based on the peaked cap used by mountain troops and featured a cloth flap that was normally buttoned up at the cap's front but, in cold weather, could be folded down and attached under the chin.

Other forms of headgear included (unofficial) fur hats, worn during the winter months on the Eastern Front, and the Army-style mountain caps for Gebirgsjäger's troops. Rather more exotic was the fez (or tarbusch) worn by Moslem soldiers. The standard fez was in field-gray, although officers wore a maroon version as part of their full-dress uniform.

Above: A 1939-pattern NCO's 'crusher' field cap with cloth peak. The standard SS death's head badge has been replaced with an old Prussian style example (without lower jaw).

Above: The ceremonial of 'walking-out' version of the fez worn by the 13th Waffen Gebirgs Division der SS 'Handschar'. For active service, a field-gray version of the fez was worn.

Right: *German officers of the 'Handschar' Division. Befitting their designation as a mountain division they are wearing climbing boots and 'Styrian' gaiters.*

ᛋᛋ *Field tunics and trousers*

The black 1932-pattern service dress worn by the Leibstandarte and SS-VT troops was found to be impractical for combat duties: it was too conspicuous in the field and also showed dirt too easily. And while the glamour and mystery of the black uniform

Left: The 1940-pattern field tunic and cap of a Rottenführer of the 17th SS Panzergrenadier Division 'Götz von Berlichingen'. The red piping on the shoulder straps indicates the arm-of-service of the artillery, while the medal ribbon that of the Iron Cross Second Class.

appealed to many SS members, those seeking to make a career as soldiers preferred to adopt a more military style of dress, which in German terms meant a gray uniform. In 1935 the armed units of the SS were issued with their own earth-gray uniform, retaining the same pattern found in the black service dress. Similarly, the Totenkopfverbände issued their personnel with an earth-brown uniform, although they were only to be worn within the confines of the concentration camp. In 1937 the German Army's field-gray was issued to all armed elements of the SS in an attempt to standardize the system, although the cut of the uniform followed the SS pattern.

The move towards the adoption of the standard Army uniform developed as war drew nearer. In 1938 the Leibstandarte began to wear Army-issue service dress and, following the outbreak of war, the other armed SS formations also made the change, mainly because they lacked an adequate supply of SS uniforms as numbers expanded. The green Army collar was retained by some units, while others replaced it with a field-gray collar.

Following Army practice, most Waffen SS officers bought their own uniforms from private military tailors, although towards the end of the war they increasingly fell back on the purchase of standard-issue uniforms from the unit stores. As a general

Below: Senior officers of the 1st SS Panzerkorps at a meeting with Hitler at the Berchtesgaden, 1944. From the left: Theodor Wisch, Max Wünsche, Sepp Dietrich, and Fritz Witt.

Left: *The cap and camouflage tunic of a highly decorated infantry Obersturmführer. Awards include the Knight's Cross (at neck), Iron Cross First Class and the Close Combat Clasp (worn above the medal ribbons). A map case and pistol holster are worn on the belt.*

rule, officers managed to maintain a sartorial distinction between themselves and other ranks as a consequence of superior tailoring, in spite of the greater degree of equality that existed between officers and men in the Waffen SS. It is interesting to note that a number of former NCOs—such as the 'Hitlerjugend' commander Kurt Meyer—continued to wear simple standard-issue uniform even after they had been promoted to high officer rank.

From 1942 onward, tunics became simpler—patch pockets were manufactured without pleats, for example, and the wool content was reduced. These economies eventually led to the introduction, in September 1944, of a new style of tunic similar to that of British battledress. Material was saved in the process, although apart from new recruits, few Waffen SS troops wore this new and unpopular uniform by choice, preferring to carry on with the old-pattern during the final months of the war.

Trousers were little altered during the war, although some minor modifications were made. The 1937-pattern straight-legged Feldhose, or field trousers, were intended for wear with jackboots; in 1942 a new pattern was introduced, called the Keilhose or wedge trousers, to fit better into the gaiters of the new ankle boots. Senior officers commonly wore riding breeches, complete with soft leather reinforcements on the seat and inside leg, although those fighting in the field tended to wear the same trousers as their men.

The Wehrmacht prided itself on the wearing of jackboots, and like their Army counterparts the Waffen SS wore the classic leather boot for most of the war. Officers, in their turn, wore slightly higher and more stylish riding boots. Even before the outbreak of war, ankle boots had been

Left: The tunic and field cap of an Obersturm-führer of the 'Totenkopf' Division. The uniform carries the awards of the Iron Cross First and Second Classes, while the death's head cuff title indicates former service in the 'Oberbayern' Standarte.

introduced within the Waffen SS but they were not popular. And when, in 1942, the jackboot was no longer an item of standard issue, soldiers hung on to them as long as possible rather than wear the ankle boots and what they disparagingly called 'retreat gaiters'.

Waffen SS mountain troops (Gebirgsjäger) wore the same service-dress uniform as their Army counterparts. This included the Einheitsfeldmütze field cap, windproof anorak and special cleated mountain boots.

One specific Waffen SS feature was the 'Styrian' spat-like gaiters that fitted over the top of the mountain trooper's boots. The traditional Edelweiss badge of the Gebirgsjäger was sewn onto the sleeve, although rank badges and other insignia were exclusive to the Waffen SS. The small numbers of Waffen SS paratroopers (Fallschirmjäger) wore standard Luftwaffe paratroop uniforms and equipment, but with Waffen SS insignia.

The Waffen SS never served overseas in hot climates, but tropical uniforms were issued in small numbers to some units, and they proved useful in the southern areas of the Soviet Union during the hot and dry summer months. These uniforms were drawn from Army and Luftwaffe sources, again distinguished by Waffen SS insignia.

SS *Protective clothing*

The Leibstandarte and SS-VT were originally issued with black greatcoats before moving to an earth-gray and then an Army-style field-gray coat by the outbreak of war. During World War II several minor variations were made to the basic greatcoat pattern, especially in the coats sported by officers; many of these tailor-made greatcoats were manufactured to individual specification, and these included extra pockets, removable linings and sheepskin or fur collars.

Although officers could buy a leather greatcoat, its cost deterred many who opted for the cheaper Regenmantel made from rubberized cotton twill—which, at least, gave it a leather-like appearance. The motorcyclist's rubberized coat also proved popular; the skirt of the coat could be divided and buttoned around the legs.

The most significant piece of protective clothing worn by soldiers of the Waffen SS was developed for their use as a result of the first dreadful winter on the Eastern Front, 1941–42. During 1942 the Waffen SS introduced the winter combat uniform (Winter-Sonderbekleidung). This uniform comprised a waterproof, fur-lined parka jacket in 'cement-gray' with matching over-trousers. The reverse side of this uniform was in white, to be worn during combat in snow conditions.

The winter uniform was improved over time and in 1943–44 consisted of a jacket (with a large hood that could be worn over a steel helmet), trousers and mittens. It was made from two layers of windproof material in between which was a wool-rayon lining. The uniform was reversible, with SS Fall camouflage on one side and white on the other. The Winter-Sonderbekleidung set a pattern for military clothing in cold conditions that was to influence the Western Allies in the postwar world; most NATO armies have worn similar garments over the last half century–and many continue to do so.

One highly unusual form of protective clothing consisted of leather U-boat jackets and trousers issued to the armored troops of the 'Hitlerjugend' Panzer Division. While in Italy, the Leibstandarte had access to stores of Italian uniforms, and among these they acquired U-boat clothing originally sold by Germany to the Italian Navy. After the Leibstandarte's return from Italy, these incongruous uniforms were assigned to the young tank crews of the 'Hitlerjugend', then undergoing training by the officers and NCOs of the Leibstandarte.

Right: *Two SS soldiers stand by a World War I French war memorial during the fighting for north-west Europe, 1944-45. The trooper on the right wears the one-piece camouflage overalls that became increasingly common towards the end of the war.*

SS *Camouflage clothing*

A second major contribution made by the Waffen SS to the development of military clothing came with the introduction of camouflage uniforms. Experiments had been made by other nations previously but the Waffen SS made camouflage a regular part of service dress for all their soldiers.

Left: The summer-side version of an early pattern SS camouflage smock. Instead of pockets it has vertical slits in the tunic sides to allow access to the field service tunic worn underneath.

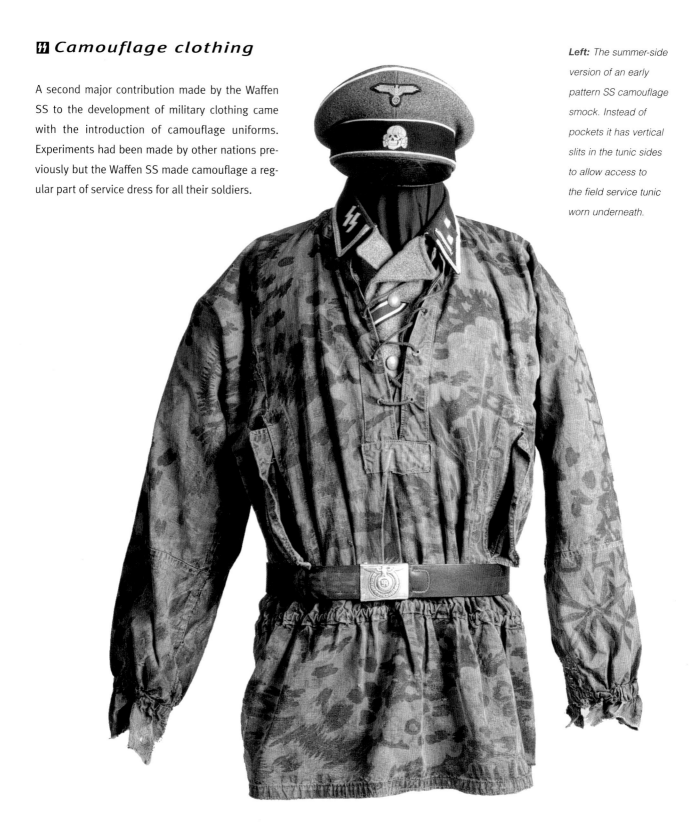

Right: A fall-side version of a late-pattern SS camouflage smock. Unlike the early pattern smock, it has pockets and foliage loops on the shoulders.

A reconnaissance battalion commander of the SS-VT and a Munich university academic worked together to produce camouflage material for a groundsheet/poncho and helmet cover which, they claimed, could reduce casualties by as much as 15 per cent. By 1938 their camouflage pattern, printed on a waterproof cotton-duck, had been tested and accepted by the Waffen SS, and was swiftly put into production. The first batches of camouflage material were hand printed, although more rapid machine printing was subsequently introduced. Nonetheless there was never enough material to keep up with demand, and camouflage uniforms remained in short supply throughout the war.

The Zeltbahn or groundsheet was a triangular piece of cloth with a slit in the middle so that it could be worn by the soldier in poncho-fashion. It could also be combined with three other Zeltbahnen to make a rudimentary four-man tent. Helmet covers were made from Zeltbahn material and attached to the helmet by a series of simple clips.

The next item of camouflage clothing was the smock, a light, loose-fitting garment of hip length, with elasticated cuffs and waist but no collar. Early smocks had simple slits in the side to provide access to the tunic worn underneath; later examples were, however, fitted with pockets and with loops on the shoulders and upper sleeves to hold foliage. The smock was a reversible garment, one side printed in predominantly green (Spring) colors, the other having a predominantly brownish (Fall) color. Although production of the smock ceased in January 1944 it continued to be worn until the end of the war. Camouflage trousers in the same design were also introduced but were far less common than the smock.

Once the importance of camouflaged uniforms

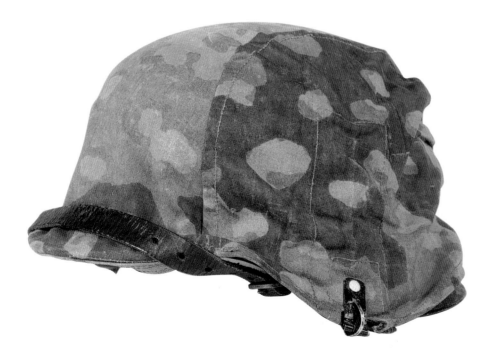

Left: An early pattern camouflaged helmet cover, distinguished by its lack of foliage loops.

was properly recognized, the concept extended to other items of uniform. The parka was issued in a brown/Fall and white/snow patterns, and in March 1944 a two-piece camouflage uniform was introduced. The tunic and trousers were manufactured from a lightweight herringbone twill onto which was printed a dotted 'pea'-pattern camouflage on one side only. This suit could be worn instead of the standard service uniform in summer, or over it in winter, although, unlike the smock, it had no waterproof qualities.

While in Italy, the Leibstandarte had gained access to rolls of Italian camouflage material which they had made up into tunics, trousers, caps, and coveralls. As a result, both the Leibstandarte and the 'Hitlerjugend' Panzer Divisions were kitted out in this German/Italian combination during the battles in the West in 1944.

Below: The M43 Waffen SS field cap, as worn by SS panzer troops in the latter stages of the war. Panzer troops had originally worn oversize berets, within which was a protective 'inner', but this had not proved popular and were replaced by field caps at the end of 1940.

Panzer Uniforms

The panzer troops of the Waffen SS took their lead from the Army and wore a black double-breasted tunic and black trousers, although the SS pattern varied slightly in detail. The Army Baskenmütze—a large, floppy beret under which was a padded liner—was also worn in the early years, although was found to be impractical. It was subsequently replaced by the Schiffchen and then the Einheitsfeldmütze field caps, both in panzer black.

Although the black panzer uniform was intended to be practical—to disguise engine and other mechanical greases—the rigors of combat suggested that some form of overall would be more a suitable garment for tank crews. A lightweight two-piece reed-green cotton-drill uniform was issued for wear by the crews of tanks and armored cars.

Right: A Waffen SS anti-tank gun crew in action. The different patterns of their camouflage smocks are evident in this photograph—as are their fluted gas-mask containers, which in the latter stages of the war rarely, if ever, contained gas masks.

This uniform was followed, in early 1943, by a one-piece uniform—similar to a boiler suit—field-gray on one side and white on the other. This latter uniform was never particularly popular because of the difficulty of getting in and out of the suit. In January 1944, a new uniform was introduced and comprised a camouflaged two-piece system in herringbone twill. As with other camouflage uniforms of the period it was of the spotted 'pea' pattern, although for reasons of economy it was unlined and was not reversible.

While tank and armored car crews maintained the right to black uniforms, the soldiers of the armored assault and anti-tank guns were accorded a similar elite status with the introduction of a field-gray version of the panzer uniform during 1941–42.

Insignia

Of the items of visual display that readily distinguished the Waffen SS from other elements of the Wehrmacht, insignia—cap badges, collar patches, shoulder straps and cuff titles—were the most significant item.

The German eagle and Totenkopf was worn on all headgear with the obvious exception of the steel helmet. On the tunic, the German eagle was also worn on the upper arm of the left sleeve, in deference to the Army, Navy and Air Force who had the exclusive right to wear it on the right breast.

Black patches were worn on both sides of the collar, and the symbols displayed differed from unit to unit. In so much as there was a standard system, most German-recruited Waffen SS formations wore SS runes on the right patch and rank insignia on the left. Some notable exceptions included the 'Totenkopf' Division, which used a death's head symbol on the right collar patch, and the Polizei Division, which wore police badges on both patches (although it later adopted the 'standard' system).

Those Waffen SS formations raised from non-Germanic peoples were not usually allowed to wear SS runes on their collar patches; instead, SS runes were worn under the left breast pocket, and a variety of national insignias were embroidered on the right collar patches.

Rank distinctions on the collar patches were indicated through a combination of stripes and pips. This system continued until the rank of Obersturmbannführer; thereafter rank was distinguished on both collar patches by silver oak leaves and pips. On camouflage uniforms, rank was shown on arm badges in a series of bars and oak leaves, printed in muted colors (green for NCOs and field officers; yellow for general officers).

Shoulder straps were based on the Army pattern and carried badges of rank. From December 1939 arm-of-service colors (Waffenfabre) were also worn on shoulder straps (and sometimes as piping on the field cap)—again based on the Army pattern. The German armed forces had a wide array of colors to match the various arms of service, from infantry to veterinary surgeons. The main arm-of-service colors used by the Waffen SS were white (infantry), rose pink (panzer and anti-tank troops), red (artillery) and grass green (mountain troops). A number of formations and units had insignia—badges or embroidered slides—which could be worn on the shoulder straps, but in 1943 this was prohibited by Himmler—although the Leibstandarte SS 'Adolf Hitler' continued to wear its 'LAH' monogram.

Cuff titles were worn by most soldiers in the Waffen SS and were both a means of easy identification and a symbol of belonging that helped foster pride in the Waffen SS. They generally consisted of a formation or unit title in white on a black background, and were worn on the lower left arm of the tunic and greatcoat. Other cuff titles included those of specialists, such as military police (Feldgendarmerie) and war correspondent (Kriegsberichter).

Left: *A selection of cuff titles worn by soldiers of the Waffen SS, from the top: 17th SS Panzer Grenadier Division; 10th SS Panzer Division; 1st SS Panzer Division; 2nd SS Panzer Division; 12th SS Panzer Division; 9th SS Panzer Division; Deutschland Standarte, part of 2nd SS Panzer Division. Cuff titles were worn with the utmost pride by Waffen SS troops, as one of the symbols that distinguished them from other SS units—and from the Army.*

Left: *A selection of rank insignia for both camouflage and field-gray uniforms. The top rows—comprising bars and oak leaves for camouflage wear—are, from the left: Obergruppenführer (general); Oberführer (brigadier); and Hauptsturmführer (captain). The field-gray insignia on the bottom row is, from the left: Oberschütze (private 1st class); Sturmmann (lance corporal); Rottenführer (senior lance corporal).*

Above: *Untersturmführer (2nd Lieutenant) Herbert Walther on his wedding day. His rank insignia is clearly displayed here, as is his old 'crusher' field cap.*

Below: *Three youthful members of the 12th SS Panzer Division 'Hitlerjugend' in Normandy, 1944. They have all been awarded the Iron Cross.*

Glossary

Allgemeine SS General SS, the main body of the prewar SS, mainly part-time members and including those not part of other branches of the SS.

Ausf Ausführung, the German abbreviation for model or mark.

Barbarossa, Operation Code-name for the German invasion of the Soviet Union in 1941.

Blitzkrieg Lightning War, the German offensive strategy that utilized deep penetration of enemy lines by armored forces, closely supported by ground-attack aircraft.

bocage The countryside encountered in the 1944 Normandy campaign, comprising high wooded hedges that were ideally suited to defensive operations.

caliber The width of a gun's bore, ranging from the 7.92mm of a rifle to a 15cm howitzer. In the German system a caliber less than 2cm is given in millimeters, above that in centimeters.

calibers The expression given to the ratio of the length of a gun barrel to its caliber, eg. the Panther tank had an L/71 gun, so that barrel length was 71 times its 7.5cm caliber. A long barrel made possible a larger charge, greater muzzle velocity and increased armor penetration.

division An all-arms formation of between 15–20,000 men at full strength, the building-block of an army.

Flak Fliegerabwehrkanone, anti-aircraft gun.

Führer Leader.

Freiwilligen Volunteer, referring to Waffen SS

units made up of non-German troops; originally those with Germanic roots, eg. Dutch and Norwegians.

Gerbigsjäger Mountain troops.

Granatwerfer Mortar, literally grenade thrower.

gun An artillery piece that fires a projectile at a relatively high velocity and a low trajectory (usually less than 45 degrees). Compare with howitzer.

Hitlerjugend Hitler Youth, a compulsory German youth organization for boys aged between 14 and 18, many of whom subsequently joined the Waffen SS, especially the 12th SS Panzer Division 'Hitlerjugend'.

hollow-charge An anti-tank projectile whose explosive charge is shaped into a hollow, inverted cone, which on detonation focuses a narrow and highly intense stream of metal and gases to cut a hole through armor plate.

howitzer An artillery piece that fires a projectile at a relatively low velocity and high trajectory (usually above 45 degrees). Compare with gun.

muzzle brake An attachment to the muzzle of an artillery piece designed to divert propellant gases to reduce recoil.

Nebelwerfer Rocket artillery, literally smoke projector.

OKW German High Forces High Command.

Pak Panzerabwehrkanone, anti-tank gun.

Panzer Tank or other armored vehicle, from the German for armor.

Panzerjäger Tank hunter; armored vehicle

whose prime function was to destroy enemy tanks.

PzKpfw Panzerkampfwagen, armored fighting vehicle; the standard designation for a tank.

Schutzstaffel Protection squad, abbreviated to SS.

Schützen Thin armor plates attached to the sides and turrets of German tanks as protection from hollow or shaped-charge projectiles; from the German for apron.

SdKfz Sonderkraftwagen, special motor vehicle; the standard designation for lighter fighting vehicles such as half-tracks and armored cars.

Sig-runen Victory runes, the double lightning-flash symbol used by the SS; worn by Waffen SS units on the collar.

Sturm Assault; used in a variety of contexts including Sturmgeschütz (assault gun) and Sturmgewehr (assault rifle).

Totenkopf Death's head, a distinctive symbol used by the SS.

Verfügungstruppen Special readiness troops, one of the forerunner units of the Waffen SS.

Wehrmacht The German armed forces (Army, Navy, Air Force). The Waffen SS was not a part of the Wehrmacht, although tactically attached to the Army.

Zimmerit An anti-magnetic paste applied to the surface of German tanks during the latter part of the war as a counter to magnetic mines.

Index

Credits

All pictures are Chrysalis Images except the following which have been credited by page number and position on the page:

TRH: 37 (top), 41 (bottom), 47 (both), 86

The editor would like to thank Paul Brewer, Katherine Edelston, Terry Forshaw, Cara Hamilton, John Heritage, and Gayatri Singh for their contributions to the production of this book.